When Surfing a Tsunami . . .

By Ziji Rinpoche

First Edition 2021
Short Moments Media: Mill Valley, California USA 2021

ISBN 978-0-9886659-8-9

When Surfing a Tsunami ...

Contents

Third Section:
Bodhicitta, Tonglen, Dzogchen, The Lineage, The Guru

Fourth Section:
Empowering One's Practice

Editor's Introduction

The years 2020 and 2021 will be remembered as a time when the whole of the world was threatened by a deadly pandemic, and many of the usual forms of human activity were limited or even rendered impossible. Fear, anxiety, loss and economic disruption were suddenly the plight of a large percentage of the world's population.

Possibly never has impermanence been made so obviously manifest to so many at one time due to one specific cause. Impermanence is the fact that all phenomena are fleeting and that they come and go ceaselessly. It is the uncertainty and insubstantiality of any person, thing or circumstance and the never-ending flow of continuous change. It is evident in the disease, degeneration, aging and dying common to any lifeform.

Another outcome of the global pandemic has been the very obvious connection that people have discovered with one another throughout the world because of the shared experience of living with this virus, and due to this shared experience, there has been an upsurge in mutual understanding, sympathy, generosity and compassion. Many, many people are looking for solutions for the suffering that so many are experiencing, and one of those generous contributors is Ziji Rinpoche, a Dzogchen Lineage Holder and a Lineage Successor of Revered Wangdor Rimpoche. She, like so many others, is eager to bring comfort and ease to beings in this enormously challenging time.

Ziji Rinpoche has been teaching for many years now and has a worldwide community of students and participants. Foremost in her Teachings is the constant pointing to the fact that all impermanent thoughts, emotions, feelings, experiences, people, places, things, worlds, universes (with all of them being termed simply "data") are inseparable from the basic state of loving open intelligence, which could also be called "strong mind," "clarity," "awareness" or any of a number of other designations which point to the ultimate basic space.

This pristine Teaching of Dzogchen, passed down as it has been over many millennia in an unbroken Lineage, is here presented by Ziji Rinpoche in a contemporary form and in a manner that is understandable to a modern person, whatever their cultural background may be. One need not have any previous exposure to Dzogchen—or any other teaching for that matter—in order to benefit from this brilliant instruction. What is more, Rinpoche's way of teaching is so practical, loving and supportive, and with only a few sentences the deepest essence can be conveyed.

The material for this book, *When Surfing a Tsunami . . .*, has been gathered from Ziji Rinpoche's talks over the last five years, and the book has been compiled, collated and edited into shape by a devoted group of volunteers. The Teachings offered here are very topical and relevant, and especially so given the circumstances that many, many people have faced during this time of the pandemic. As the title implies, no matter what afflictive circumstances there may be in one's life that have to be dealt with, the power of the Teaching will carry one through.

The first section of the book introduces the core Teaching of the inseparability of open intelligence and data, how to rest as open intelligence, and how to have freedom in immediate perception. The second section looks specifically at various aspects of impermanence, such as economic uncertainty, disease, aging, degeneration and death. The third section introduces the Dzogchen Teaching more specifically through chapters on Bodhicitta, Tonglen, the Lineage and the Guru. The fourth offers instructions in empowering one's practice, with the final chapter being the culmination of all the other chapters, laid out as it is with key points and pith instructions.

A few practical notes might be helpful as the reader progresses through the book. The key terms: open intelligence, strong mind, data/data streams, resting, reification—along with some other unfamiliar terms from the Tibetan tradition—are defined in the text. The introductory chapters (Chapters One through Five) are meant to be read as a cohesive whole, and the narrative thread flows from one paragraph to the next. However, in Chapters Six to Twenty, those chapters consist of separate outtakes, which while similar in theme to the others in the same chapter, are meant to be read as self-contained teachings, which are separated from one another by the symbols of the dorje and dilbu illustrated here below:

We, the editing team, want to express our gratitude to Ziji Rinpoche for her many compassionate and skilled contributions to the benefit of all, and we are most enthusiastic about bringing this incredible wisdom Teaching to a broader audience, especially in this present time where it is so very much needed. Great good fortune! Great good fortune! Great good fortune!

First Section

GAINING CONFIDENCE IN LOVING OPEN INTELLIGENCE

AN INTRODUCTION TO OPEN INTELLIGENCE, STRONG MIND

CHAPTER ONE

Open intelligence—strong mind—has always been our only reality, and it always will be our only reality, whether recognized as such or not. Wherever we are, open intelligence/strong mind is; wherever open intelligence/strong mind is, we are. We are unborn open intelligence; we always have been, we are now and we always will be only that. There is no destination anywhere in sight.

Open intelligence is the power to know, and the power to know—knowing itself—is the exact nature of open intelligence. Open intelligence never comes together nor separates from anything; it does not come together with us nor does it separate itself from us. There is not a single thing anywhere that can be found to be apart from open intelligence.

To introduce open intelligence very directly, stop thinking just for a moment. What remains? A sense of alert knowing that is open like a clear sky. This is the pervasive, inexhaustible and undistracted singular intelligence that knows, sees and does. Our own knowing is that itself, so how could we possibly be apart from it?

Open intelligence already is. It does not require being or doing in any certain way. Even when we are sleeping, dreaming, unconscious or dying, the reality is that we are never apart from open intelligence. Open intelligence is in all things, without there being separate "things" in which it could exist. By living as open intelligence, we live in basic harmony with all, and this harmony is not something that is contrived. It comes from the realization of equalness and evenness. What could be more harmonious than equalness and evenness—the reality of everything.

"Data" is a term that can be used for all thoughts, emotions, sensations, experiences, people, places, things, which are in fact nothing other than the dynamic energy of open intelligence. To rely on thoughts, emotions and sensations—data—is the learned activity of the mind that drives us into a life of reification. We learn to reify thoughts, we learn to reify emotions and we learn to reify sensations and experiences. "To reify" means that we give people, places, things, thoughts, emotions, sensations and experiences an independent nature. Hence, these data are seen to be real, and the open intelligence which is their true essence is overlooked and ignored.

Prior to knowing any other way to be, the reification of thoughts, emotions, sensations and experiences has informed everything we do. This is what is called "the worship of thoughts, emotions, sensations and experiences." It is to take all the data that are available and to decide that this is what we are and how we will identify ourselves. Most often we don't realize that we have even done this or that we could be something other than this.

No one wants to live in a continuous emotionally embattled state, but when we think that reifying thoughts and emotions is all that we've got, then we go ahead in that direction. But when everything is left *as it is*, we're leaving the *dynamic energy* of open intelligence *as it is*, no matter what we might be calling it. By leaving the dynamic energy of open intelligence *as it is*, profound wisdom, aspiration and action to benefit all is released.

The inexhaustible open intelligence of love, which is the mind of great bliss seeing emptiness, is what open intelligence is. Each of these—spontaneous great bliss seeing emptiness, strong mind, open intelligence, love—is the same. They're all equal. There are many names, but what is most important is the practice and the realization—upon introduction, practice and realization in the moment, without waiting for something to come about somewhere down the line. We *are* open intelligence and love. That is our actual nature, and there is nothing that we need to do for that. We don't have to earn it; it already is. It is simply a matter of realization.

"Open intelligence and love" and "strong mind" are terms which serve to communicate to the greatest number of people in the world of today. In some teachings the word "intelligence" alone has been used, but to give it a more decisive meaning, the word *open* has been added to it—*open* intelligence, an intelligence that is open. And then also, not an abstract, unfeeling and distant open intelligence, but open intelligence as *love*!

Many people think of intelligence as closed within their body, but that simply isn't the case. Open intelligence is simply *as it is*, the intelligence that is the basic state. It is, again, an open intelligence, inseparable from love.

OPEN INTELLIGENCE/STRONG MIND, INSEPARABLE FROM WISDOM

Whatever thought, emotion, sensation is present, that is where open intelligence is. That is where strong mind is. Wherever strong mind is present, open intelligence is present; wherever consciousness is present, open intelligence is present. There is only open intelligence, and that's it!

Open intelligence is all-seeing, and all sound whatsoever is the primordial sound of open intelligence, no matter what we might make it out to be. The feeling of "I'm thinking," or "I have this sensation of sight or fragrance or hearing," is open intelligence.

Open intelligence is inseparable from profound wisdom, and profound wisdom is what makes sense of everything.

Our natural resource is in open intelligence. Whether we are happy and carefree or writhing in pain and misery, this is the resource we want to train up in. Our natural state of unborn humility is our go-to and our take-away from life. Instead of trying to construct a life in the context of reification, now we can live as seamless benefit and empowerment of the space of open intelligence, strong mind.

There is no need to hide from anything; we can experience all data totally. Wide-open intelligence and love release tremendous energy, which is usually constricted by the process of trying to control the flow of data. In fixed reference points there is a retreat from the direct experience of everyday life which is always flowing openly and beneficially as open intelligence. When we feel ourselves under assault by afflictive emotions, they can appear to us like a tsunami of negativity.

But instead of being overwhelmed and washed away by it, what if we remained as the open intelligence that is in fact the basis of the apparent tsunami? What if, instead of drowning, we were able to surf that tsunami, no matter how powerful it appeared to be, through resting as the peaceful equalness and evenness of open intelligence that is inseparable from the data that appear? What a magnificent life that would be!

Completely open intelligence triggers joy and the energy of benefit and connection; however, this goes unrecognized when we focus only on data. By the power of open intelligence, there is complete openness to all data, without restriction or limit. This openness automatically outshines the barriers created by emotional and mental patterns.

The essential nature of all data is enlightened open intelligence. The mind of all is enlightened open intelligence. The life of all being is also enlightened open intelligence. In enlightened open intelligence there is nothing relative or absolute.

Open intelligence is not bound by the tension and contrivance of hope and fear and outshines the hope and fear of looking for great results. Open intelligence destroys the self-promoting confines of artificial conduct. Open intelligence transcends meditation and non-meditation. Calculating activity and non-activity dissolve in pure space.

As It Is

Letting data streams be as they are is what "*as it is*" means. Everything just simply is *as it is,* and there's no need to dive in and try to change it or to make it better in some way. *As it is.* In letting everything be *as it is,* we find that data spontaneously self-release, and we don't really have to do anything for that to happen. Every single moment self-releases, and every data stream self-releases. All this is the display, the dynamic energy, of clear-light open intelligence.

It doesn't matter what the data streams are, we can just let all of it be *as it is.* We let the data streams self-release on their own. Everything self-releases as pure, bright space, and is itself pure, bright space. If some other reification comes up, it too self-releases, and it isn't connected to the former one. The idea that the former might be connected to the latter is just a made-up story.

If you are ruminating about lots of things, wherever the rumination is, open intelligence is! What's really key is that open intelligence be foremost in the rumination. The rumination as such just does whatever it does. It's a matter of habit, and by bringing open intelligence to it, you change the habit, and the rumination naturally settles down. By bringing more open intelligence to the ruminations, the dynamic energy of wisdom and compassion are more available.

Stormy feelings go on by, and like the flight path of a bird in the sky, these feelings disappear. Where did they come from? Where did they go? They're the energy of open intelligence. Open intelligence is present, strong mind is present, but not as a thing, not as a subject or an object. Instead of focusing on data, the focus is open intelligence; that's it.

There are only two choices: to focus on maintaining open intelligence or to focus on data. It's a choice to empower oneself—or not. It's completely up to all of us to make our decision in each moment.

RESTING FOR SHORT MOMENTS, MANY TIMES

CHAPTER TWO

No matter what happens, there are two choices: to rely on open intelligence, or, to perpetuate the story of appearances. That's it. Whether the appearances are conceived of as being mundane or special, in either situation there is an equal opportunity to realize the nature of one's own being. We don't need all kinds of ways to realize open intelligence. Actually, nothing is needed.

When the terms "rest" or "resting" are used, they mean to allow short moments of open intelligence, many times, leaving everything just *as it is*. Short moments increasingly open up the balanced view, clarity and insight of open intelligence. Short moments repeated again and again become spontaneous, and clarity becomes increasingly obvious until it is evident at all times. We gain deep confidence in the power of short moments to bring benefit to our lives.

We keep it simple: resting, or we could also say "relaxing," for short moments, many times. If we have positive data, that's fine. If we have negative data, that's fine. There is no need to control the natural flow of data. Rest. Relax. Place the emphasis on short moments of open intelligence instead of on data—that's it! The data just flow along doing whatever they do. Open intelligence is naturally at rest. Leave everything *as it is*.

A short moment of open intelligence eventually grows longer and longer, until open intelligence is obvious at all times in our everyday experience. The first time the choice is made to rely on open intelligence—rather than emphasizing data—there is a sense of complete relief that is to be found in resting as open intelligence. By persisting over and over again in this one simple choice, very clear benefits are seen.

Resting for short moments, many times, as open intelligence allows us to become familiar with open intelligence. We grow accustomed to leaving everything *as it is.* When we're strengthening open intelligence, it does not mean that we're trying to get rid of data. Strengthening open intelligence is realization of the *indivisibility* of data and open intelligence. Data are the dynamic energy of open intelligence; data are the dynamic energy of profound wisdom and of the aspiration and action to benefit all and to enlighten the collective. This is a very important point.

Prior to the introduction to open intelligence, strong mind, *we are practicing reliance on data*, and there can be lots of things that provoke us—that poke, poke, poke us. But in short moments of open intelligence repeated many times, the poking is outshone, and no longer are we feeling down-pressed all the time. World civilization, with the exception of sublime practitioners, is down-pressed, op-pressed and de-pressed, but as we practice short moments, we come to see everything in a completely new way.

Resting for short moments, many times, is really key—just short moments without trying to add anything else to it. External, internal, future, past, present, none of it is worth thinking about. We rely on open intelligence, allowing everything to be *as it is,* even if we are having all sorts of thoughts with lots of internal self-criticism, such as, "Should I be doing this practice? Am I doing it right? Is this good for me?"

In practicing short moments again and again, open intelligence and love become obvious. They are in fact *already* always obvious, but not yet obvious enough to someone who is devoted to reification! They are obvious enough when there is only wisdom and love that is directed towards the enlightenment of all right now.

Through short moments of practice, we naturally find that we become familiar with the clarity of the nature of mind. Writing out texts, reading texts, listening to talks—all of this is a form of becoming more familiar with short moments.

It isn't necessary to go "over there" to enlightenment and then bring it back "over here." We don't have to go anywhere; we just relax with whatever is appearing. Some of us have wild mental states and others of us have practically none, and then there are those with all kinds of things in between. Just relax. It all is *as it is,* and there is no distinction. An expansive equalness and evenness—this is our true nature, not something that is just for special people or for only a few.

First, there is the introduction to open intelligence, strong mind, then the introduction is practiced without doubt. That means that even if there is doubt, short moments, short moments, short moments. Not in the way of, "Doubt, oh dear, oh dear, oh dear," but rather, "Doubt, hey, so what?" Practiced without doubt, complete assurance comes about. That is the foundation for saying, "Wow, I'm exalted; we are all exalted." Exaltation is the nature of human beings. So, no matter what our doubts or intellectual dilemmas are, the practice of short moments brings bliss to everything, no matter what it is. There already is bliss, so it is just a matter of clarification.

YOUR ULTIMATE REALITY BECOMES OBVIOUS

In this Teaching the ultimate result—the fruit, as it were—is introduced in the beginning. There isn't a process of working up to the fruit; it is the fruit itself from the very beginning. In short moments your ultimate reality—*our* ultimate reality that we share as one open intelligence—becomes more and more obvious. Short moments is the easiest of all practices, and it's also the practice for the people who are most capable of practicing, the people who are considered to be of most excellent and superior openness.

When you practice the short moments meditation, you are associating moment-by-moment and more and more with the vastness of your own open intelligence and love from which all power comes—the power to love, the power to be generous, everything. So, you choose short moments. Even in the face of a tsunami, you rest and choose short moments; you surf the tsunami. This is what will carry you through.

At the moment of the appearance of whatever data are arising, you could go off into elaboration; however, in resting as open intelligence you find the wisdom to see things as they actually are. Even if you should go off into an elaboration, continue to maintain open intelligence. Open intelligence isn't separate from the elaboration, but in order to gain stability, it's important to rest as the elaboration arises. The resting stability has to be developed before it's possible to maintain open intelligence in the presence of an elaboration. Resting eventually burns off elaboration until there isn't any elaboration, and whatever occurs can be seen clearly *as it is*. Then appropriate action can be taken, if necessary.

The practice of short moments is based on *quantity*, not quality. Any kind of perception of quality is subjective, so it means nothing. Since we never know what conditions will bring, the only way to be with the impermanence of data is with strong mind for short moments, many times, repeated over and over again until open intelligence is obvious. Then we can feel confident that we have what it takes to be anywhere, anytime. Drop by drop, the *quantity* of short moments is important, not the quality. Whatever the ups and downs, whatever the tsunami may be—quantity, quantity, quantity. Quantity, not quality, because quality is impermanent.

It could be that experiences of bliss, clarity or non-thought come and you think, "Oh, I've got it. This is it. Finally, I'm enlightened," but this kind of experience is not realization, because it is impermanent. We hope so much that it will be permanent when it happens, but then when it isn't, we're disappointed. So, once again to repeat, *quantity* of short moments, not quality! These short instants are not timeless, and they're not-not timeless; they're not time, and they're not-not time. Just rely on short moments without trying to figure it out, and more and more everything will open.

We have come to see, possibly in a painful way, that our hopes and fears aren't really leading us anywhere. If we're lucky, once we recognize this, that's when we begin to question things. Otherwise, we grow old and we just feel regret. There is regret about the past, but we don't really know exactly what it is we regret. Instead of that, there is resting for short moments, repeated many times. Short moments is really key—just the short moments without trying to add anything else to it.

Most of us know on some level that we can't control the people around us or the unfolding events of our lives. The more we rest one-pointedly, radically and without any recourse to anything else, the more we realize that we can't control people and we can't control the events of our life, because they are totally impermanent. So, we rest radically. We rest as that which offers all love and all intelligence. If we are unhappy, we can't blame anything or anyone for our unhappiness, but we can never see that fact clearly unless we rely on open intelligence. That's our source of total clarity and of total honesty.

Given the state of infinite evenness—open, relaxed and spacious—there is no sense of practice, for there is no distinction between short moments and the periods in between. Everything is unrestricted, completely equal, uninterrupted and shining open intelligence. Shining open intelligence is focused and demonstrated in qualities and activities which ensure full enlightenment of the collective quickly.

Do not ever believe that a short moment of complete relaxation is meaningless. It is our cure-all and savior, and it is that for everyone else as well. It is not a cure-all found elsewhere nor a savior who lives up in the sky or somewhere else, but it is *us* as the savior of self-release from the knotted-up notion of self.

A DEEP UNDERSTANDING
OF THE TEACHING

CHAPTER THREE

The true nature of mind is "the mind of great bliss seeing emptiness." The mind of great bliss seeing emptiness is always already present; it is simply a matter of recognizing and activating it. Through this recognition the mind is expanded vastly, and its focus is much different than the way it had been focused before. Maybe the focus for our whole lifetime has been on the reification of data. Reification is what we have been taught and what we have learned and taken on. We learn it in order to fit into the group of humans who believe in reification, and this is what almost all do and how almost all live—the reification project!

In order to make the mind of great bliss seeing emptiness obvious, first we need to be *introduced to open intelligence*, then we *practice without doubt,* and then *complete assurance comes about*. Each of these is directly related in succession to *view*, *meditation* and *action*. The *view* is open intelligence pervaded by love—pervaded by not just any love, but by ultimate love. The *view*—loving open intelligence—is introduced and illuminated in the very beginning. We don't wait around to be enlightened; from the beginning we're shown to actually be enlightened. Enlightenment is clarified for us; we know what it is. We also know that *we* are responsible for our own data streams and that they are not the responsibility of someone else.

First the *view*, then the *meditation*, which is the practice of resting for short moments as the view—without doubt. What that means is that even if doubts come up, one keeps practicing. *Meditation*—resting for short moments, resting moment-to-moment as the *view*.

View, *meditation*, and *action*. *Action*, or conduct, is wisdom exaltation and sublime enlightened energy of mind, body, speech, qualities and activities. This is the mind, the speech and the body of enlightenment. As we practice, our mind is guided by pure perception, and with that our speech and our conduct change without any effort. Complete assurance comes about.

One must distinguish between ordinary intelligence, which is conventional or commonplace energy, and open intelligence, which is enlightened energy. Ordinary intelligence is just constant words and thoughts going on in the mind, with sensations and other things going on with the body. It is feeling like *we are* the body and the mind, and that everything is inside the skin-line, along with the feeling, "That is what I am." Ordinary intelligence is also the under-mutter—the things that we don't even know that we're thinking about—but then once in a while we catch ourselves in the under-mutter.

How then is enlightened energy different from this ordinary energy? Ordinary energy is informed by reification, and enlightened energy is not. It's as simple as that. The more we build the foundation for enlightened energy, the more likely it is that it will become more obvious, and the more likely we will have a solid foundation in open intelligence. From that solid foundation we have indestructible dignity and sublime enlightened energy. This is how it is distinct and vastly different from ordinary behavior. In enlightenment the behavior is informed by wisdom, and the actual activity is skillful means— so, wisdom and skillful means together.

We have been trained to see dualities everywhere we look. However, there is no duality. Duality and nonduality are conceptual frameworks, so there isn't any need to get rid of one and take on another. They are both data streams. Open intelligence itself is profound wisdom. Everything we've ever wanted to be is in open intelligence. We can't conjure up profound wisdom through virtue and through other meritorious activities. It only is in already available open intelligence. There's no way to conjure up the will to benefit all or to enlighten the collective. It isn't something that exists in conceptual frameworks. Rather, it is the outpouring and the emanation of open intelligence.

THE GREATEST SERVICE WE CAN OFFER

First, we have to have a deep understanding of the Teaching. Then by practicing resting for short moments, we begin to see everything *as it is*. No longer do we think data are something that are going to take over our mind and make us depressed for years; instead, we see data *as it is*—open intelligence pervaded by love. We leave it *as it is* without going into the agony of depression or anger or whatever it might be.

From that we begin to have pure perception. We see everything as pure—our thoughts, our own body and mind, the trees, the birds, the whacky leaders of countries, the good leaders of countries, viruses—all pure perception. This is because our focus is enlightenment; it isn't political renewal or changing the world. What is the best way to change the world, the most aggressive political action one could take? Enlightenment for all right now. To be able to see everything as pure and to be committed to the enlightenment of all is one form of the "surfing the tsunami" that we have been speaking about. Surfing, rather than drowning, comes from the clarity of perception that naturally arises from seeing things as they truly are.

When we come to the point where we're spontaneously leaving everything *as it is* without thinking about it, it becomes easier and easier for us to have pure perception. By leaving everything *as it is*, we come to see that the positive data don't help and the negative don't harm. This is a significant realization. We open up to pure perception, and we come to see *everything* as pure perception. When everything is purely perceived, we open up to truly radical compassion, a compassion that goes beyond everything we might see individually. Radical compassion, complete heartfelt love.

The greatest service we can offer is to maintain pure perception, to have a deep understanding and instinctive recognition. Based on that instinctive recognition we actively practice pure perception. Then there is total release, and everything is seen as dynamic sublime energy, vast and spacious. This is the case.

Everything that appears is illusory, it doesn't matter what it is. It doesn't matter whether it's an object of experience, a data stream, or say, your perception of being a subject that perceives an object. Whatever the cause and the effect are, both are equally illusory. What is not illusory is the all-accomplishing wisdom of open intelligence.

The more we realize open intelligence, the more we are convinced that even our own humanness is an illusion, even though to say this may sound preposterous to many people. Open intelligence is always present, and because humanness is seen to be an illusion, *our practice matches what human intelligence actually is*. At one time I didn't realize human beings were an illusion. I had questions though, because I knew that everything was made of subatomic particles, so I knew that people couldn't really be a singular solid entity. They had to be a part of a field of energy and that this was probably a more likely ultimate reality.

Open intelligence—strong mind—is always present from instant to instant. To expect it in the future is a mistake, because there's no observable future. It's always right now; there's only right now. If we think about the future, it's only right now. If we think about the past, it's only right now that we're thinking these thoughts. Time and timelessness too are observations; they're experiences, they're not realization. All of these conceptual frameworks do not represent what open intelligence is in itself.

They are an emanation or an aspect of open intelligence. We don't know why things are the way they are; all we know is that we want to practice!

WHAT IS ENLIGHTENMENT?

What does "enlightenment" actually mean? Often a definition is not given when enlightenment is spoken about, but I would like to tell you exactly what enlightenment means in terms of being a human being. It means the demonstration of profound beneficial energy in mind, speech, body, qualities and activities. That's what it means. When we talk about enlightenment of the collective, that is exactly what enlightenment of the collective means.

Over time enlightenment has been described in many, many ways and increasingly so now with the wide reach of the Internet and the very large number of books on the topic; however, what has been described as enlightenment has been tarnished by so many misinterpretations. One way that the term has been misunderstood is that enlightenment has been described as only belonging to certain historical figures, time periods, countries or cultures. Enlightenment has also been considered to be a thing, a destination or a place to go, and that one would look a certain way and have certain definitive marks and behaviors once one is enlightened.

However, enlightenment is not a destination, and illuminated intelligence doesn't have to look any particular way. Enlightenment doesn't need to be grasped. There's no place to get to, for a balanced view has no destination. Everyone has already always arrived! The word "enlightenment" needs to be brought into a commonplace nomenclature, which is much better than dressing it up in old garments that are ready to fall apart anyway!

There are a number of different types of enlightenment, so to speak, and many of them have to do with self-centered enlightenment, which is enlightenment for a seeming self. However, in reality this is not a self-centered pursuit. There will eventually be a realization that there is no self to be realized or enlightened. True enlightenment is the enlightenment of illuminated intelligence, where illuminated intelligence benefits all.

The idea, "I am going to get enlightened for myself," is a very small space to live from. There are many qualities and activities of what could be called enlightenment that are very much needed in this world, and many people around the world are saying, "I want a new way to look at the world that is not self-focused." The internal preoccupation with "I, me and mine" can come to an end.

"I, me and mine" may be present in a certain sense, because first we have to say, "I really am interested in enlightenment, and I want the best means of enlightenment available." But when we no longer hold realization to be purely for ourselves, we reach a crucial juncture where we don't even think about "my realization" anymore. The enlightenment of all beings is at the forefront, and whatever we do to ensure the enlightenment of all beings, we are ensuring the enlightenment of ourselves, because after all, we are already one of those beings that we are striving to enlighten! "All beings" would include us, and that's a very profound realization in itself.

ENLIGHTENMENT IS PERMANENT HAPPINESS

At one point I realized I was completely open and that I wasn't confined at all by anything—and neither was anyone else. That was the immaculate concept of inexhaustible benefit, the primordial unborn source. "Unborn" meaning "primordial," never born, never entering into any kind of process, such as being born, living and dying. Unborn, always *as it is*. There is no way to undo that. The only refuge in life is the refuge of open intelligence, the refuge of this perfect love that we live in, of, as and through. That is the only reality of who we are.

Before pearls have been strung on a string, the pearls are laying scattered here, there and everywhere, and we can only see them as something separate. The more we practice short moments, the more the data streams—the "pearls"—become strung together in a continuous display of open intelligence with no interruption. What seemed like divided points of view are seen now as brightness and as great bliss.

A lifetime of worry—for some people that is their practice: worry, worry, worry, worry. But as for myself, what I am "worried" about is the enlightenment of all, right now! That's what I'm focused on. Do you want to worry about that with me? And actually do something about it? There's a difference between worrying about it and actually doing something about it.

Everyone, no matter who they are, longs for permanent happiness, permanent happiness that will not go away. There isn't anyone who has tried to be happy and then reached a plateau of happiness, feeling, "Oh thank heavens, I'm now happy and it will last forever," because of course this sort of happiness doesn't last forever. Enlightenment *is* permanent happiness. That is what can be said about enlightenment—permanent happiness, no matter what goes on in one's life or in the world, no matter what tsunami may come. This is what will carry you through.

DEDICATION AND DILIGENCE

CHAPTER FOUR

These particular Teachings are for people who are best suited to them. The Teachings are simple and direct, and some people are attracted to them and others aren't. That means simply that some belong in this Teaching and others belong somewhere else. Just like if you were studying physics and someone else was studying chemistry, you would be in different classes. It is the same here; there are different skillful means for different people to become familiar with enlightenment.

Short moments of leaving everything *as it is* is the practice that is easiest for some people to open to the nature of mind, but that does not mean that *only* people for whom it is easy can realize open intelligence. With the right personalized tools, anyone can have the evocation of open intelligence.

What exactly is a practitioner? A practitioner is the one who practices, the "person" who is the actual basis for realization becoming obvious. The practitioner is someone endowed with all the freedoms and advantages and who has faith and compassion. That means that the practitioner has the freedom and advantages to actually use their strong mind to inform all actions. They use their strong mind, instead of using a mind that's scattered all over in stormy feelings.

I use my strong mind every second of the day. Every second of the day I rely on my strong mind and I think about my Guru, Wangdor Rimpoche, because *he is equal* to my strong mind. By looking at *his* great qualities and activities, that's the only way I can see my own. Each of us has a brightly shining sun inside ourselves, and that brightly shining sun is our strong mind—open intelligence. It's like millions of brightly shining suns shining from within our heart.

The teacher introduces a student to open intelligence—strong mind—in a way that the student can actually realize it. It is made clear enough that eventually there is a stable foundation in open intelligence, and whether that occurs in the beginning or occurs later, whichever way it is, that's just the way it is. There is no one else with the very same data streams, no pool of data streams exactly alike for each person. Each is swimming in their own stream, yes, but opening out into the vast ocean.

Enlightened energy is always already present for everyone, but it takes someone to convince us of that. Because we are raised to believe in self—self-protection, self-sustenance, self-criticism—enlightened energy can be very remote in our perceptual field. It just isn't known to be there, because we have been taught to reify everything. However, a master can cut right through reification with their words and their presence, even if they don't really need to say that much.

Each of us practices devotion to something, whether we realize it or not. For instance, we might be devoted to our self-identity, or we're devoted to the way we look, or we're devoted to differentiating ourselves from others. This is what we're trained to do in what could be called "reification boot camp." What is reification boot camp? It is the training from the very beginning of life to rely on reification, and then to have it drummed into us over and over again throughout life.

Reification means that we don't believe in open intelligence; we believe that everything is independent from any kind of universal intelligence and that it has its own intelligence and is separate from whatever that universal intelligence is. But, does it make sense that our intelligence could be separate from a universal intelligence? No, because if it's universal, it *pervades all of us,* and it pervades all of the many worlds that are proposed to exist.

ASPIRATION AND ACTIVITY

The attitude with which we need to practice is one of dedication and diligence. We have to have the aspiration and then the actual diligence to practice. Diligence means that whenever we don't feel like practicing, we do it anyway. So then, two other aspects along with dedication and diligence are aspiration and action. Aspiration is the intention, and then action is the commitment and the actual diligence to train in the practices.

Profound wisdom is always indivisible from the aspiration and activity to benefit all, to enlighten the collective. There isn't any moment that is dissociated from that. The fuel for this is aspiration and activity—the qualities to benefit all, to enlighten the collective. Through introduction to open intelligence we can proceed with confidence and without doubt. Whenever any doubt comes up—"I don't think this really works," or "I don't feel very openly intelligent today" or whatever it might be—it's a doubt, and the resource, the solution, is already present as strong mind itself.

Once one has an introduction to open intelligence, it needs to be practiced in order to be realized. So, *real-ized*, made real. Say you have a few days or even a few weeks of some kind of incredible state and you think, "Wow, this is it. I'm down with this direct realization thing!" Then all of a sudden, something comes up out of the blue—the bank statement or the child screaming their head off or whatever it might be—and then you draw a blank. Everything that seemed so obvious in your subjectively defined idea of realization has disappeared.

And yet, whatever the experience is, open intelligence and love are spontaneously present in *all* experience. It is the everyday intelligence of all experience—eating, breathing, disturbing emotions, working, playing, going to the toilet, making love, panicking—everything! There are so many things that we might think are mundane or even frightful. "Oh no, that couldn't possibly be loving open intelligence." However, *everything* is included and subsumed in loving open intelligence, including the tsunamis! This attitude of strong mind makes the surfing of the tsunami so skilled and easy.

Whatever is going on, there's nothing to change. Everything is totally relieved. Thoughts are outshone on their own just by the energy of wisdom and love itself. It doesn't matter whether we think we're the best practitioner who ever lived or the worst; there's no distinction whatsoever. Everything is *as it is*—an expanse of equalness and evenness.

THE FOUR MAINSTAYS

"The Four Mainstays" are the core support structure for anyone interested in gaining assurance in open intelligence. The Mainstays are 1. The practice of resting for short moments, many times. 2. The trainer. 3. The training. 4. The worldwide community. The Four Mainstays are the passageway through all afflictions old and new. It is important to rely on short moments and the key points and pivotal instructions given by the trainer. The training media will reveal exactly the instruction that is needed at the proper time, and the worldwide community supports a lifestyle of relying on open intelligence and its beneficial potencies. In a Four Mainstays community we are amidst a group of people in which we can find good friends, who have already been through what we are going through and who are very willing to support us in any situation that will arise.

Through a Four Mainstays lifestyle we come to have the immediate benefit of open intelligence as our firsthand knowledge—not as an intellectual object of attention, but as a full heart-response. We rest as indestructible great outshining and inexhaustible open intelligence, perfect love, perfect knowledge and perfect capability. It is important to recognize that the practice of short moments and the Four Mainstays lifestyle is ongoing. It is involved in every single thing we do. It isn't only one thing, like just the short moments practice; it is a complete lifestyle.

With the Four Mainstays we elect a lifestyle that will deepen and further the practice of gaining assurance in open intelligence. When we make a one hundred percent commitment to this lifestyle, it is not a contrived commitment. It is the full-on acceptance of the commitment of open intelligence's beneficial potency *as it is*—the only reality of what we are.

Special, rare and precious are the Four Mainstays because they are ultimately reliable and are there for us as a source of complete joy and comfort. And yet, if we have no familiarity with them or confidence in them, we cannot possibly understand their benefit. It is supportive to reflect on the potency, exquisiteness and rarity of the Four Mainstays—the gift of practice, trainer, training and community—and to be aware of their power and what they bring to the human community across the globe.

RECOGNIZING STRONG MIND

If you have been introduced to strong mind, maybe you recognized it as the *you* that you truly are, even though you may not have previously called yourself that. You possibly recognized something about yourself that had been unknown, and you knew that that is where you can rest. This is all part of the faith and compassion for yourself—faith in yourself and compassion for yourself.

All-accomplishing wisdom means that whatever is needed in the moment is exactly what happens. It doesn't happen from elaboration of thoughts, emotions and sensations; it happens from the clear shine of open intelligence. Just like the light of the moon shines equally on everything, so the light of strong mind shines equally as all of its dynamic energy. There isn't anything excluded; everything shines equally. To be naturally endowed with faith and compassion is a tremendous gift.

If we just look at the community of practitioners, we can see that being kind is a way to bring happiness. Being kind is a way to be happy! When we are kind, it is like a brightly shining sun; we rely on our kind mind, we rely on our shining mind, we rely on our strong mind, and through that we are spontaneously kind. Not "kind" in a Pollyanna, sappy sort of way, but spontaneously kind, giving whatever sort of kindness that is needed, whether it's wrathful, peaceful, or as it is most of the time, in between.

In each time, place and circumstance, whether there is the conceptual framework of time or not, there is perfect knowledge of what to do and how to act. Not only is there perfect knowledge, but there is great cheer in being alive as this perfect knowledge itself. We have taken ourselves to be reified mind, speech, body, qualities and activities, but these are the fleeting appearances of liveliness through which we know ourselves to be in, of, as and through loving open intelligence.

Open intelligence—strong mind—is sweet, fresh and always new. We are never going to be able to escape the inexhaustibility of the pure space of benefit that we are. We are endless. If there is any fear of inexhaustibility or endlessness, well, you might as well face your inexhaustibility right now!

Because human beings are just now coming to be introduced to the most comprehensive order of knowledge, we can't really imagine what is to come. We might be able to imagine it a little bit, *but it will be much better than that*! I can tell you that. I know that whatever I imagined about my life and what it might be, it's much better than any imagined concept.

FREEDOM IN IMMEDIATE PERCEPTION
CHAPTER FIVE

When data appear, we rely on open intelligence. When data do not appear, we rely on open intelligence. This is the know-how of resting as open intelligence. Data vanish naturally, leaving no trace. In the simultaneous occurrence of open intelligence and data, open intelligence is intense and enormously potent. To see unerringly that data and open intelligence are inseparable is to have freedom in the immediate perception of the flow of data, with no need to change the data in any way.

No matter what shines forth, there is complete perceptual openness in all experience, freedom in immediate perception. This is a carefree mode, wherein data simultaneously shine and outshine as open intelligence. Without the entanglements of hoping to achieve open intelligence and fearing that you will not, or hoping to avoid data and fearing that you will not, the prison of hope and fear collapses and there is no thing called "open intelligence" to strive for or achieve, nor fear of lack of achievement. There is potent, all-beneficial openness and evenness, without any effort, without anything needing to be done.

Leaving everything *as it is* is essential, because there really isn't any open intelligence to get to or any data to get rid of. Freedom in immediate perception is the most fortuitous of gifts. There isn't anything better in life. There is no greater fortune. This is the reason that open intelligence is called "the wish-fulfilling gem."

If you have already been introduced to open intelligence, the key point then is to leave everything *as it is*. It is important to relax as the vast expanse. The body-mind itself is a data stream, so just let all the data streams—the thoughts, the sensations, whatever they are—be as they are. In this way, open intelligence shines brighter and brighter.

Instinctive recognition has two parts. One is the practice of bringing open intelligence to everything that appears. This is called awareness *as it is*. No matter what appears—open intelligence is *as it is*. No matter what we've called the data in the past, open intelligence is predominant. Anger, desire, pride, arrogance, envy, jealousy—all of these, *as it is*.

The second opening in instinctive recognition is pure perception. It is everything *as it is* with deep understanding, which allows the opening of pure perception. No matter what we see, it is pure. There is no longer a notion that something is right or something is wrong; instead, everything is now absolutely pure exactly *as it is*. There's no need to make anything out of it or to go one way or another. This is absolutely required for the opening into the totally sublime energy of wisdom.

Freedom in immediate perception does not mean that, "Okay, I'm free in immediate perception, but then something comes up and I'm not free, and then it disintegrates and I'm again free in immediate perception." The point of freedom in immediate perception as a practice is to realize that it is equally and evenly pervasive in all experience, including in all of the intense data streams that we have been calling tsunamis.

The first time that there is an instinctive realization of a pith instruction—rather than merely an intellectual understanding—it is extremely profound. "Complete perceptual openness in all experience" is one of those instructions. When we hear about this for the first time, even though it may have a ring of truth, we may not be able to understand it. Then perhaps we get a little more instruction, and we come to see in our own experience that complete perceptual openness and freedom in immediate perception have moved from intellectual understanding to instinctive realization. More and more the instinctive realization builds, builds and builds. It isn't that it wasn't there and now it's building; it's just that now we are recognizing it, that's all.

All places and circumstances are the riches of sublime enlightenment. Whether we are in the most polluted city, a beautiful park or a jewel palace, sublime enlightenment is all-absorbing of all perception. Even though a circumstance may appear to be "dirty," it is not so in enlightenment's sublime eye. All is sublime without any effort, without anything needing to be done.

Second Section

RESTING WITH IMPERMANENCE

In this upcoming chapter and in the chapters following it (Chapters Six to Twenty) the material is presented in a slightly different way than in Chapters One to Five. Rather than the text being in a narrative flow from beginning to end as was true in Chapters One to Five, in the following chapters and through to Chapter Twenty, the text within the chapters is divided into separate, distinct teachings (which could be one or two or even more paragraphs in length).

While similar in theme to the other teachings within the same chapter, these separate elements are to be read as stand-alone teachings, where there can be a slight pause and possibly a bit of reflection and contemplation before moving on to the next teaching. These separate bits are divided from one another by the use of graphics—the symbols of the dorje and dilbu pictured below—which serve to prompt pause and reflection.

THE LAW OF IMPERMANENCE APPLIES TO EVERYTHING

CHAPTER SIX

No matter what appears, it will change and eventually vanish naturally. The law of impermanence applies to everything. What hasn't yet appeared will appear, and whatever appears will disappear. The things that were appearing at one time have all vanished, and now there are other things appearing.

The whole world could blow itself up in an instant, but indestructible open intelligence would still be, so why not get familiar with that? When you know this, where is the need for fear?

This is definitely a time for any practitioner to see what a blessing it is to be aware of impermanence and to see that impermanence is simply the energy of strong mind. The only energy we have is strong mind. Nothing is anything else other than strong mind, so forget all the labels. Impermanence is the mind of great bliss seeing emptiness.

We as practitioners are so fortunate to have been prepared to face a high level of impermanence—and daily increasing impermanence. This pandemic that we are facing is not something that is going to go away in a month or two. The only way to approach the entire circumstance is through the recognition of impermanence.

In this pandemic, very similar things are going on all over the world, and all over the globe we're in a common situation. So, right now it is so important to rest. That's the option that is very different from being completely afflicted by what is going on: resting, and then experiencing the comfort that comes from resting naturally. There isn't any other place to go. To revert to the past when it seemed like it was much better or project into the future about what might happen, well, we don't know! We don't know! That is the beauty of impermanence: we don't know.

Certainly, life on earth has probably seen worse pandemics than this, but I really wouldn't know if that is true or false, so it's simply an assumption. But you know what? I don't really care about all of these opinions, except for discovering in this and in all things what can be offered for the benefit of all. These or any other opinions are not specific things to focus on; they're all energy—the energy of exaltation for the benefit of all.

No matter what any of our individual attitudes might be, we need to practice impermanence, because anything that we've seen or experienced so far that has been stunning or surprising or gives us a nudge like, "Oh no, what's going on?" just know that that will continue and that it's part of world suffering. We as practitioners already know that the world is in a state of suffering, so that isn't a hurdle we have to get over. Practitioners already know about impermanence, so what a blessing that is right now.

Many of the things that are occurring are shocking, and for most people they will not be able to be revoked. That means: be prepared. And be prepared to start surfing whatever tsunami is coming at you at whichever moment it may be! No one is out of the picture; no one is out of the scope of what is occurring. What is occurring is only more impermanence; it's just that it's so glaringly obvious when everyone is acknowledging their suffering together.

As long as someone does not accept the fact that data are impermanent, and as long as one does not give up clinging to data as though they were permanent and real, the mind of great bliss cannot possibly be born in the active mind of that person. Emptiness isn't a thing; the mind of great bliss isn't a thing. However, it's obvious; strong mind is a very, very obvious realization that only pours forth the benefit of all.

If we just think about our bodies for a minute, we see that everything about us is impermanent. The hair that is growing out of our heads right now isn't the same hair as what was growing ten minutes ago. All the cells in our body change; after some time we have all new cells comprising our body. This is the fact of impermanence. However, the human body, like all other data, is actually comprised of open intelligence. Every single thing about the changeable human body is open intelligence.

Data are subject to the law of impermanence. So, no matter how much positive data we have—we could have all the money in the world, all the houses, all the right circumstances—this would never ever counteract the uncertainty or surprise of some kind of colossal negative data. So, again, the skilled surfing of the tsunami comes from fully realizing that everything that arises and resolves is impermanent.

"Bodhicitta" is the all-pervasive, all-consuming desire for the benefit of all. The attitude of Bodhicitta is that we are mind's pure nature, which is called clear light. Clear light is the mind of great bliss seeing emptiness. It is not a thing; it is a realization, a *realization*, real, real, real, real in every single moment—realizing the mind of great bliss seeing emptiness. In impermanence is emptiness. Impermanence is the evidence of emptiness. We're born alone, and we die alone. None of our friends or family can go with us, nor our possessions or wealth; all of these things completely disappear, and there's only the mind of great bliss seeing emptiness.

In recognizing it now, we will know how to be when we die. We know how to truly be—the mind of great bliss seeing emptiness. This is the resolution of impermanence. We're taught through reification that things are *permanent*, but any of us upon examination of our own life can see that from one second to the next everything is impermanent. It's impossible to replicate what happened a moment before.

If we examine reification with the scientific method and ask if things have an independent nature, no, they don't have an independent nature. Not even the Higgs boson has an independent nature. As many of you know, physicists built the enormous linear particle accelerator through which they hoped to find the Higgs boson, and they did find it, but what are they left with at the end of this search? The scientists are always looking for something smaller, and this search will go on and on.

But how about starting with reality *as it is* and going from there? The discovery of the Higgs boson only led to looking for some smaller subatomic particle, because this is the way the scientific method proceeds. These discoveries are of course notable, but they are also impermanent. What is the permanent discovery? Open intelligence is the permanent discovery!

Regardless of the total length of life, in each instant life is running out. The recognition of this impermanence is very important. Impermanence and death. If you want to think about something, these are the two to think about all the time: impermanence and death.

BY KNOWING THAT THINGS ARISE, WE KNOW THAT THEY CEASE

Only open intelligence is stable and permanent, and anything that is fleeting is impermanent. This is something I would request that you reflect on: impermanence as it relates to birth, life and death and your very own birth, life and death. Impermanence.

When I was a young girl and I began learning about civilizations, I became fascinated with the ancient Indus River civilizations. All the buildings there were made of sandstone, but due to strong and sustained winds, the buildings were worn away and became smaller and smaller, until they just returned to the desert. Impermanence. To constantly have impermanence in mind is a very good practice. Impermanence motivates practice; death motivates practice.

It isn't necessary for anything to disappear for it to be impermanent. If we really stop and look carefully, we can never say exactly when something appeared or when it disappeared.

From the vantage of open intelligence, we can see that whatever it is we truly are subsumes appearance and disappearance.

By knowing that things arise, you know that they cease. By knowing that they cease, you understand impermanence. By understanding impermanence, you realize genuine emptiness. Knowing that apparent reality is empty of itself, let accomplishing and rejecting dissolve. Knowing that genuine reality is empty of other, let go of fixation on achieving some result. The mind, free of trying to do anything or stop anything, is blissful, open, spacious and relaxed. How delightful to know the whole host of reification to be self-liberated. How brilliant it is when all reifications are self-liberated.

The lack of substantiality or permanence in all that surrounds us can give rise to unhappiness and pain, as so much of our life has been based on our reified training that we need to create something substantial and permanent in life. We are driven by this very convincing training that tells us that we have to create something substantial and permanent, when in fact everything is insubstantial and impermanent.

We may be trying to hold onto something or make something stop or get something as an antidote, but whatever it is, just rest and stay still. Stay still just as you are. Do not cling to anything as though it were real. Reflecting on the truth of impermanence is very important, as it helps put strong mind in the position to really want more of itself, rather than wanting something else. Having understood the impermanence of everything and having entered strong mind, attachment to a lifestyle of supposed permanence is reversed. It's not just taken a little bit away, it is reversed. Contemplating impermanence again and again stimulates faith in strong mind.

Once my Guru, Wangdor Rimpoche, said to me, "Westerners think that enlightenment is in the mind, while Tibetans think enlightenment is in the heart. But in Tibet, when we throw a body up on the hilltop, the buzzard that comes to peck away at it doesn't care whether it's the mind or the heart." An excellent teaching on impermanence and an excellent teaching on emptiness.

BEING ABLE TO ADAPT TO ANY SITUATION

From the time that I was a small child I have been so tuned in to suffering and to the world's physical and mental pain, and I became interested in how to respond to that. What came to me through the process of practice is that the best possible response is enlightenment of the collective, and there's no way for enlightenment of the collective to occur unless that happens for each one of us. That's what it means—enlightenment for *all* beings.

Once that complete commitment is made, then all of the opportunities and the tools come into being for it. They're magnetized for that to happen. These are very powerful ways of being, and so vastly more powerful than reifying everything. To reify everything is very primitive, so we now are launching into a new way of being, a very glorious and gracious way of life.

People think, "Well, I have time. I'll get around to practicing by and by," but life goes past very quickly, and so at least a little bit of desire to practice now is necessary. In order to raise and support that feeling of urgency, you need to meditate a bit on impermanence. No matter how much you have cared for your body, it will eventually be food for fire or buried in the earth.

When the death of the physical body occurs, you will be separated from all the things that you have ever loved. Just as you were born alone, you will enter death absolutely alone. It is necessary to spend some time thinking about this, for contemplation on death is a great form of meditation on impermanence. Both the "highest" and the "lowest" experience impermanence, every single one. There is no one among you who will still be sitting here a hundred years from now. So, you need to think about this a little bit.

Sickness and misery. At some point we all have sickness and misery, and yes, I've had those, too. In a world of impermanence, there is no way to avoid sickness and misery. That's another thing that's very important about a firm decision to practice without doubt, because if we give in to doubt, then we end up miserable and afraid. It is of course good for us if we know how to handle sickness and decline, but if we don't know how to handle it, then we just kind of go down the drain through the reification of all the things involved with the misery of sickness and decline. The reification experience doesn't have anything to do with who we really are. Rather than going through life—and death—in this way, it is so much more exciting to be able to be with the experience from the vantage of open intelligence.

All appearances are a friend, a soothing friend. We have to be able to adapt to any situation, especially to those of impermanence and to realize how these are friends of practice. If we practice strong mind and reflect a lot on impermanence, then we actually experience the great realization that all the enlightened energy of data is equal to the mind of great bliss seeing emptiness. If we have just a small run-in with impermanence, we get a small bit of realization, but if we have a *big* run-in with impermanence, we get big realization! So that's why, seen from the vantage of open intelligence rather than reified thinking, impermanence is a friend along the way.

THE END OF SUFFERING

CHAPTER SEVEN

If we just have descriptions and ideas about everything that is arising, without maintaining open intelligence, we will most likely be unhappy, even miserable. Another word for that is suffering. Buddhism talks about "the end of suffering," and this is really what enlightenment is—the end of suffering. "The end of suffering" is a way of saying "enlightenment." When there isn't all the obsession with happiness and sadness, then we rest as the most comprehensive order of intelligence.

The Teaching points to the fact that suffering is never caused by the things themselves; rather, we have been trained to believe that happiness can be obtained through things that are only ephemeral and transient—like a great house to live in, lots of money and material goods, the right clothes, a partner, kids, and so on—but all these are impermanent and insubstantial. It is very important to emphasize the fact that the suffering we experience is not because of these things in themselves, but due to our misconception of them.

We are taught to think that if we just fix this thought or emotion or obtain this thing or that thing, we can avoid suffering. We think that if we are smarter, prettier, wealthier, more powerful, living somewhere else, younger, older, male, female, with different parents—you name it—things would be different. But even with the fulfillment of these desires, things are not different ultimately.

If it is said that "suffering is empty," what does that actually mean? It means that suffering is in actual fact the energy of emptiness. Although "the energy of emptiness" can be defined in many ways, in this Teaching we use the term "loving open intelligence," and we allow all knowledge to flow from that.

"Enlightenment" can be an overused and misused word; however, I think almost everyone can understand the expression "the end of suffering." There can be an apparent end-of-suffering where the thought comes, "Oh boy, I'm so happy today. I know I'm going to feel this way forever," but then soon thereafter the next thought comes, "Oh no, I have the coronavirus. This is really serious. I am so upset." So where is the happiness then? This is the type of happiness that is impermanent. Impermanence—all of life is impermanent.

Suffering is guaranteed from beginning to end if we don't hear about enlightenment and consider it deeply. Or maybe we hear about it and we're in a circumstance where everyone else around us is realizing enlightenment and we just can't take advantage of the situation. So see, there is even suffering that is related to wishing for enlightenment! Here we need to simply have a relaxed attitude, a way of rest, and whenever enlightenment shows its face, we can recognize it and rest, knowing everything is okay.

The mind that sees all of this going on is the mind of great bliss; there's no separate mind of great bliss stored in a distant house that we can't get to. One could say that the suffering is all our own, but just like suffering is all our own, we find that enlightenment is all our own, too.

The desire for experience is the fundamental cause of suffering.

Suppose that someone says, "You're no good, and I'm going to tell everyone about it!" Usually when a person hears something like this, they have an emotional response. At that moment, due to the desire for experience, that usually serves as a prompt to elaborate on it. "Oh dear, they think I'm no good and they're going to tell everyone about me. This is terrible; how am I going to deal with this?" As soon as this emotional response takes place, at that moment, rest. Do not go into the desire for experience. Rest and leave everything *as it is*. This is the place of unexcelled wisdom exaltation and sublime enlightened energy and the real end of suffering.

To see that we suffer is a very simple concept, and it's very easy to accept the concept of suffering when we first come upon teachings that tell us about it. "Wow, I can really relate to the fact that I suffer, and I can make a list of all the ways that I suffer. I worry about money; I wonder if I'll always have a place to live. I wish I had the money to treat my sick pet." Or, it can be at the far other extreme: "I have so much money that I don't know what to do with it, and I don't know how to take care of it. I feel so incredibly stressed and inadequate to the task." Suffering can take all kinds of forms.

Each of us has an individual idea of happiness. This individual idea of happiness is very unique to us; there is no other person who has the exact same idea of happiness that we do. One person might have happiness related to career achievement, another might have a notion of happiness related to being a good parent, while someone else might have the notion of happiness that includes neither of those. Whatever the view of happiness, the happiness is fleeting. Just as the idea of suffering is fleeting, the idea of happiness is also fleeting.

When we come to the Teachings, we come to actually recognize that we all share something fundamentally in common—our experience of suffering. With that recognition, we can come to be kind to ourselves. In being kind to ourselves, in recognizing our own suffering, we recognize the suffering of others as well. We see that what is true for us is also true for others.

When there is pain of any kind—the pain of aggression, grieving, loss, irritation, resentment, jealousy, physical pain—if we really look into that, we find out for ourselves that behind the pain there is always something we are desiring.

The truth of suffering is not a doomsday prediction; it expresses the fact that we are not being aware of what we really are. In the moment of suffering, rest completely and radically as the open intelligence that we truly are.

It doesn't matter why this all came about, where it came from, what it is or anything else; none of that matters. All that matters is realization and wisdom; that's it. That's what strong mind is. It's the experience of strong mind—its realization, its wisdom exaltation and its sublime enlightened energy.

It is not a matter of practicing to diminish suffering or to enlighten everyone sometime in the future, but enlightenment of all *right now*. By practicing for the enlightenment of all right now, it holds us to account for our own practice. Some are attracted to giving their life to ending suffering, but to practice "for the enlightenment of all right now" is the way to bring an end to suffering. To practice in this way is very rigorous and requires a great deal of self-reflection and examination.

CHERISHING SELF-IDENTITY

We suffer because of our mistaken belief that we are a separate, independent, solid "I." However, our practice eventually becomes such that we don't operate any longer from the idea of being separate and independent and a solid "I." For each of us, we have our own reified way of looking at things and a reified way of describing who we are, but the need to be unique and the need to stand out as an individual is also a cause of suffering. It is important to know that the perspective of enlightened energy does not come from focusing on that place of a separate, independent, solid "I."

We are trained to cherish self-identity, to build a unique identity that differentiates us from others. "This is who I am. I do this, that and the other thing. These are my friends, and these others aren't my friends. This data I like, and other data I don't like." That's likely what we have been trained in, but we have a much easier time of it when we are seeing things through the clear perspective of open intelligence. Building a unique identity takes a lot of work and can never be satisfied, and it is an endless pit of despair.

So, with our need to be special and unique we can say, "Okay, *no* to that! Now I trust open intelligence, and I allow my self-cherishing identity to absorb completely into open intelligence, because I don't want to fool with the other things that I've been trained to perceive." This is the easiest way to live.

Suppose I have some kind of idea about an identity that I want to achieve in order to feel special and unique. Maybe I go on to a good university and then get a graduate degree, and so I'm better educated than most people. Then I get a grand job and some kind of career that's incredible and earn a lot of money. But if one really looks at it in a clearheaded way, it is still a matter of being hungry, hungry, hungry.

Nothing is ever good enough for the self-cherishing identity, and it's such an exhausting proposition to keep sustaining it. Life is much easier when we allow everything to be absorbed into sublime awareness. That's where the real power is: sublime awareness, inexhaustible perfect knowledge. We have our choice: desperate self-cherishing identity or enlightenment identity. What is it going to be?

OUR REIFICATION IS TEMPORARY AND SUFFERING CAN END

The end of suffering is the end of the desire for experience. Instead of running with the desire for experience, one rests as the essence of everything. Resting. One's life commitment in terms of ending suffering for oneself requires the commitment to end suffering for everyone. There can be no wisdom exaltation and sublime enlightened energy without this firm commitment. "In this lifetime, right here, the end of suffering will occur for everyone"—that kind of commitment. The enlightenment of everyone. There is no reason that it can't happen, as everyone is enlightened already!

Because it is unrealistic to hope for a completely stress-free life, it makes more sense to learn how to deal with the stresses that inevitably arise. This is the beauty of short moments, which can be practiced twenty-four hours a day. Even if we sit in meditation for long periods of time, still the ongoing practice—in sitting meditation as well—is short moments, many times. This is so rich because we know from the beginning that the practice relates to all aspects of our life, not just the periods when we are sitting in meditation.

The good news is that our reification is temporary. It is like mist in the air that easily burns off in the bright sunshine. Open intelligence—strong mind—is the sunshine of our mind. Therefore, suffering can end, because our desire for strong mind is always available to us. We don't end desire as much as we say, "Hey, I'm going to desire something that works, something that really brings me the love I've sought." This is the end of suffering. By living ethically, practicing the meditation of short moments and developing wisdom, we can take exactly the same journey to enlightenment and freedom from suffering that the buddhas do. We too can wake up.

"Buddha" in this reference is not limited to a person or a historical being; buddha is qualities and activities. Everything is the vast expanse of buddha—of buddha body, speech and mind. So, the word "buddha" means not merely an enlightenment of mind, but also an enlightenment of speech and body, with wisdom exaltation and sublime enlightened energy. What need is there to mention striving for the welfare of all without exception, when everyone already is a buddha?

To end suffering means that we bring about an enlightened collective. The beginnings of that are in retraining our mind through the Twelve Empowerments (*the foundational training in this Teaching*), where we see that past, present and future are actually the mind of great bliss seeing emptiness. We're not reviewing our past from a psychological or sociological perspective; we're seeing that everything is Bodhicitta mind, seamless mind, equal and even. Bodhicitta—the all-pervasive, all-consuming desire for the benefit of all.

All knowledge, whatever it is, is already present. It's already present, and what is called "human intelligence" did not create knowledge. We have been trained to believe that humans construct knowledge and intelligence. However, humans do not construct knowledge or intelligence. Humans are simply discovering what is *already available*—all knowledge—like a miner in a gold mine. From sublime awareness we know that all knowledge is already present. The outpouring of perfect knowledge that occurs within sublime awareness isn't seen as something earthshattering. We may be awestruck in the face of it, but it is not something that is earthshattering. In one way it is, but in another way, it isn't at all. It simply is what actually is.

Fortunately, simply by being a superior or most excellent practitioner, you are born to great fortune, born to a sublime life, no matter when you first recognized that it is sublime. One comes to be able to joyously say, "Wow there is a way out! I can relax and take it easy. I can enjoy the things I want to enjoy, and I can do it with others who have the superior intention to enlighten all beings." Because it's enlightenment of *all* beings, "all" includes us as well! We don't have to work on ourselves solely, because we are practicing to benefit all. As enlightenment is all-inclusive and all-pervasive, every act of ours is inclusive of all—and of ourselves. That's good too—inclusive of ourselves and indestructible! There isn't anything to understand or accomplish. So, we relax completely, knowing there's nothing to do. Rest is best.

There is no wisdom exaltation until ordinary thoughts come to a complete stop. For most of us, the way that this is realized is that first we notice that our mind has calmed down a lot. For those whose minds have calmed down a lot, it's very easy just to relax and let everything be *as it is* when we feel an emotional grip.

I have all kinds of thoughts! But I don't have ordinary thoughts. For me, suffering has ended. That's all I will say—suffering has ended. Suffering is not, and suffering is not-not, but you will never realize this through a lot of thinking and conceptual analysis. Only through practicing short moments of open intelligence pervaded by love will you reach a point where you know suffering has ended for you. Then you have the powers of buddhahood. Then you have ultimate compassion, which is called Bodhicitta. In suffering there is no suffering. Like I said, it's not and it's not-not.

IF THE WHOLE WORLD
FALLS APART

CHAPTER EIGHT

It may be that you have an incredible flood of feelings about all of what has been going on in your life, and yet, it's possible to eventually come to the point where you can have a good chuckle about the way you have been deceived by reification! But that chuckle isn't possible as long as you go after all these descriptions and try to shape them in some way so that everything makes sense, because it never will! It really never will.

It's difficult to not have the data of being upset with the state of the world today. Despite the constant assault of the media telling you about how bad things are, as data occur, just allow everything to be *as it is*. As these points of view of extreme negativity, anger, hopelessness, powerlessness, loss of revenue, loss of jobs, loss of food to eat and loss of place to live are appearing to you in the context of a pandemic—as occurring in the present or perhaps occurring in the future—don't try to control them in any way. If you rely only on the antidotes you come up with to deal with the anger and fear, you are just going to take yourself down. If you find yourself going into a full-fledged panic attack as a result of this upsurge of impermanence-data, by far the best choice is to root yourself in strong mind.

We all can see that there are many choices about what we're going to do with our lives, like for instance with relationships—whom to be with, how to decide, when to decide and all of the emotions that go along with these choices. There are also concerns about a career; we can look high and low, and endless careers present themselves. Financial concerns, that's another one for almost everyone. "I need money to eat and to put a roof over my head and maybe I won't have enough." All of these present endless concerns about life.

As practitioners, we need to place our focus in the vast expanse, because without open intelligence, any of the areas I just mentioned will be fraught with endless sorrow. This is just the way it is. The more that qualities and activities match the wisdom essence, the easier it is to be in life. This doesn't mean that we cannot have a career, get married or be together with a partner, or handle money expertly and well. The point is that all of these are much easier from the vast expanse, because the vast expanse has the all-encompassing view, not just a narrow focus.

When we have the intention and motivation to commit to shining open intelligence, and when we further inspire that intention and motivation, which has hitherto been fractured through engagement with reified things, and when we settle on shining open intelligence as the core of our entire human experience, then all of these juggling balls of career, finance, relationship, family and everything else all just settle into place. Everything becomes much easier. A great way to approach what goes on in life is to not need to obsess about it!

What's most important is that when we look at our choices in life and when we have a decision to make, we ask the question, "What will be of greatest benefit to all?" This is a question I have asked myself throughout my entire life in making decisions. "What will be of greatest benefit to all when I make this decision?" I use that for everything. I use it for my financial decisions, for how I'm going to spend my time and who I'm going to spend my time with. "How will this be of benefit to all?" It's a greatly powerful decision-making tool.

Only in spontaneous comprehension of our blissful truth, only in the spontaneous devotion of selfless love, only in affection and indivisible intimacy is there the openness of our all-pervasive transmission. Attempting to establish control through data streams—money, power, prestige—is futile. There is no way to establish control through any of these means. There will always be the desire for more money, for more power and for more prestige, if that is the road one chooses.

Some people seek power through notoriety or money or whatever other means, but there is never enough fame, power or money. Any kind of seeking of comfort through any means whatsoever ends with more seeking—for more power, for more money, for more privilege, more knowledge, more intellectual understanding. All of this is nothing. Only in open intelligence is there true power, and that is the power to benefit all. That is true power. All power, all money and whatever else people might seek is stripped away at some point, and at death it will all surely be stripped away. There is no amount of power or money that can comfort a dying person—none. Only the perfect love of open intelligence comforts all in all situations. This is the reality.

No matter what happens, a river just keeps flowing. I don't know how many of you have seen the Ganges up in the Himalayas in India. It is incredible what that river goes through—all of these rapids and waterfalls and enormous dams, and then finally it flows for thousands of miles and out into the Bay of Bengal. People are putting all kinds of things into the river, and it just keeps flowing, no matter what's in it.

There isn't anything in open intelligence, by the way. It's brilliantly empty of anything other than itself. The more that this becomes obvious for us, when we come to the time of our death, nothing else other than open intelligence is obvious. We don't even have the data stream of life anymore, not even a tiny memory. Gone completely, as though it never happened. Just like when we wake up in the morning from the dreams at night— never happened! Cool, huh!

THE SKILLS FOR HANDLING MONEY

Money data are the call of open intelligence, calling us to untold riches—not to work harder to make more money! By letting the money data be *as it is*, the door to the open intelligence-treasury opens up, and its all-providing energy replaces the exhaustion of making money and accumulating things. Instead, super-beneficial body, speech, mind, qualities and activities are filled with open intelligence's potency devoted to all, providing without limit or restriction the skillful means that are required.

The surety of open intelligence replaces the constant mental muttering about finances. In simultaneous receiving and giving, we are released from a constant sense of lack and imperfection into prosperity and infinite generosity. In this way, even the data about sickness, aging and death are the vivid potency of all-soothing, extremely potent open intelligence, like the force of the ocean is inseparable from the ocean itself.

It's important to build the skills for handling money, and we have teachings on that. Building the skills to handle it is a very important foundation for having money. It means that you know what to do with it, just like with anything else. Suppose someone gave you a tool as a gift, but they didn't tell you anything about what it was or how it is used. One must become familiar with the tool and its proper use. Same with money.

As we never know what's going to happen, we want to prepare ourselves with what can endure any experience. Financial unreliability is not going to go away, so we need to discover the best means possible to deal with the circumstances that we will be facing. When we see that we've had excessive reactivity to something that has no independent nature—like money—then we can just relax in the face of that reactivity.

That doesn't mean that we stop working at our jobs, keeping track of our investments or that we disregard the fact that we need to save for our retirement. We want to know that, by the time we are seventy years old, we are not on the dole or living some other way we don't want to live. We want to know that we have taken care of ourselves and that we have supported ourselves in this life. No matter what our money lifestyle is, we are paying attention in a relaxed way, informed by open intelligence.

Most of us learn to hoard money. The worshiping of self-identity and the worshiping of money are simple data streams. By relaxing totally and completely in that instant of completely open intelligence, its immediate benefit is realized. We have a direct experience of the inseparability of open intelligence and benefit, and that's what we can really rely on.

There is a man I know who inherited many millions of dollars from his mother, and this vast inheritance didn't at all change his fears about not having enough money. Not only that, now he has the worry about having to take care of all that money. That is a lot of work; that's more than a fulltime job! Through the wisdom eye, we're able to see, "Oh gosh, whether I have money or don't have it, there is still the worry about money!" The need to worry about money is just another training we have received in the data-reification boot camp.

Suppose fear about money comes up again, and then pretty soon, "Oh, I'm thinking about the past and not having money, and then thinking about the future, because even though I have money now, I probably won't have enough in the future," and so on. However, with past and future outshone, everything is already given right here; everything we possibly need is already here. Through the wisdom eye, we're able to see this clearly. When data of what is external and internal are outshone, open intelligence shines. There's no longer thinking about, "Oh, that's going on in here, and that's going on out there." Internal and external are outshone, and the vast expanse is now the perspective. Before and after, past and future—all gone.

Today in contemporary society we have an economy of exchange. It means that if I give you something, you are expected to give me something back. If, for example, I am selling you a car, then you are expected to give me something in exchange for purchasing that car. Whether it's realized or not, this is not only based on having something to buy or sell in exchange for money, it's also the case in our actions in general. "If I do such and such, then I expect an exchange from you. If I love you, I expect you to love me back." That's often what is anticipated and hoped for.

I recently said to someone, "At one time I thought about earning money, but that seems like another lifetime." I never think, "Well, I need to do this so I can earn some money." That is not where my mind goes. I just show up wherever I am, and then whoever contributes, contributes, and then I have food, clothing, shelter, healthcare and education. I have everything I need. I have no desire for anything beyond what I have. Please know that by fully and completely living as open intelligence, you will live without ever thinking about "needing to earn money" as the cause of you doing whatever you're doing. Rather, the benefit of all becomes the cause of you doing what you're doing.

I once had a very large amount of money due to me that I was counting on to carry me through, as I had depleted all my other resources. Guess what? The money never came through! What did I have? I had zero dollars, *and* I had the potency of open intelligence. I had no idea how I was going to pay my rent or pay for food or anything, but I thought, "Well, beneficial potency is what I'm committed to and I'm staying put. I'm not going to move off course, no matter what."

Just out of the blue things started occurring by their own force. I was renting the place where I was living, and the people who owned it said, "Oh, just go ahead and live there as long as you need to." So, I lived there for two and a half years and I paid nothing, as they were paying everything. They didn't even know what I was working on, but they just knew somehow that whatever it was I was up to must have a force of its own. I did eventually pay them back all the money for rent and utilities; even though they didn't want it, I gave it to them. Somehow it all worked out, and everything was fine, and everything *is* fine.

If I had run off course and had started doing other things to try to create money, I would have been unable to put all of my energy and commitment into this wonderful movement that we all have. That's just from my own experience; this is what actually occurred for me.

Generosity with money might be the way that we start to expand the amount of beneficial potency we express, but that is only one form of generosity. Generosity is considered to be the foremost of all uncontrived virtues, because we are *innately* generous. First of all, we can be completely generous with ourselves by allowing ourselves to know our true identity. We expose ourselves to everything we can that will shine more light on our true identity and that will enhance, enrich and support the radical reality of our true identity. This is a great generosity, and that generosity allows us to connect with all beings. Instead of fending off most people and trying to draw close to only a few who might seem safe and comfortable, there is complete openness to all beings and indivisible relating with all beings. Wow, now *that* is an expression of true generosity!

WHAT WE CAN COUNT ON

Our primary identity, one that will never change, is the basic state of open intelligence. No matter what appears within the basic state—our birth, our life, our death—the basic state remains unchanging. That is where we want to gain confidence, because it is this that we can count on. We can't count on conventional descriptions, and in the midst of a global pandemic, this has become very clear, hasn't it? There needs to be a new way of understanding the nature of things. However, this doesn't mean that one way of thinking immediately collapses and then right after that collapse another arises. No, it is in the coincidence of the collapse of the old and the appearance of something new that there is a very powerful shift.

Rather than being distracted by all these events that we are experiencing in the world now, root yourself in open intelligence. If the whole world falls apart, open intelligence is what will carry you through. Yes, indeed, when surfing the tsunami that is breaking upon the world these days, open intelligence is what will carry you through.

Life without ups and downs is inconceivable to most human beings, and ups and downs are based on believing that thoughts, emotions, sensations and other experiences have some kind of power to cause the effect of "ups and downs." That is a fundamental misunderstanding. What appears within the basic state never alters the basic state in any way. Regardless of these descriptions, the basic state is unwavering—never altered or changed in any way.

Aren't many people looking for some kind of success? However, even if you have a career that leads to success, how good is that career going to be to you on your deathbed? Will you be reading contracts and paying bills on your deathbed? No, all that goes away. So, it's important to rely on the identity that is truly findable, the one that is ever available.

Get familiar with what is real and forget about all the silliness and make-believe! Why go along with all these ideas that have never worked for anyone? Instead, grow in familiarity with open intelligence. In resting more and more you will come to know who you truly are, and more and more you will be able to handle all situations without impediment. You will be able to do things you could never have imagined doing, and this will occur to you naturally and effortlessly. Ways to make the world a better place that will astound you and astound others will come from just letting the powerful current of open intelligence be *as it is*, with no need to impose descriptions upon it.

Even if during my lifetime the United States has been quite well off, who knows what might happen in the next years? We in the United States have lived with such privilege, and I think that this is one of the reasons that in this country there is a culture of self-indulgence, in which the point of life has been to indulge the self in different practices, like becoming somebody important who will be noticed—that kind of thing.

But along with the idea of being an individual self who wants to be somebody, there can also be the idea of living life for the benefit of all. This is an aspect of the highest wisdom, but it isn't taught in culture generally.

The benefit of all as expressed in your own life is really based on what you most like to give in life. Whatever you are most happily engaged with and what you most enjoy doing is your way of being of benefit to all. By deciding on it, making a commitment, then moving forward step-by-step, it becomes your gift of highest wisdom.

THE GREATEST TREASURE

When you find your peaceful nature in yourself, that experience can't be matched by anything in life. That's the greatest treasure you will ever find in life. There isn't anything greater. You could have all the money on earth, all the finest foods or whatever else you're looking for in the world, but none of it can even come close to your peaceful nature. Your peaceful nature will take you all the way. When you're on your deathbed, that's all that's left.

By relying on peace, you make the best investment you can make; it is an investment with no downside and only upsides. You know that you've found what really works. When you see all those things that you used to rely on collapsing all around you—and you still feel strong, peaceful and happy, and that you want to reach out and help someone else even though the whole world is collapsing—that's when you know that your peaceful nature is yours for the having.

The political and economic authorities of past and present have led us to where we are today. That shows that there is a basic misunderstanding about the nature of reality. It's all going to fall apart at some time. I've always said this, even if many were probably thinking, "Oh, I used to think she was a little strange when she would talk about the banks and economies collapsing," but, hmm, guess what? We want to prepare ourselves, because we never know what's going to happen; we want to prepare ourselves with what can endure any calamity.

Strong mind is what we really want to fortify ourselves with, and not with more eye-candy, ear-candy or touch-candy. Instead, we need to find what is at the basis of all the senses. What about us is so fundamental that it permeates all sensations, something that is equally present in our sensations during the day and when we are asleep at night? All our experience of waking, dreaming, sleeping, the experience of being born, living, dying, it is all fired by our peaceful nature, by strong mind. Timeless awareness, strong mind.

"Oh, man, I have all these afflictive emotions that are coming up for me!" None of that stuff is going to go away, by the way, so you don't have to worry about missing out on anything! You'll still have the same old problems that come up in your thoughts, emotions, sensations and other experiences—at least for a while. Until you start to realize that they are all saturated with your peaceful nature, they are going to keep cranking out. But whatever they are, there is nothing to be afraid of, nothing to hide out from. Why be afraid of yourself? There's no way to get away from *you* as you truly are!

The powers of great benefit provide beyond anything that could be comprehensible intellectually. They provide great fortune of the material kind, and they provide great fortune of the mental and emotional kind. This great fortune of the mental and emotional kind is what we see most immediately. We see upon introduction to open intelligence that we have found a great fortune. No longer do we have to pick through the garbage to try to find some good garbage. Instead, we see that actually all of what we've been picking through is in fact pure gold! All of it is the power of great benefit.

No matter what your woes might be, whether they're woes about money, sickness, a place to live or a job—woes I have faced as well—it's time for everyone to face up to the reality that it is only in open intelligence's great benefit that we have the power to overcome the forces that seem to be in our way.

To say that we are exalted creatures is not just a concept. Instead, according to the highest wisdom, it is the *fact* that we are exalted by nature. We are exalted by nature, period. As we live our lives embraced by that wisdom, we see more and more of that exaltation, and the more the exaltation, the greater the humility. They just go together. Life is so incredible and filled with gift after gift.

There are all these motivational speakers who say you can have everything you want and that they are going to show you how to get it. That kind of astounding occurrence can happen sometimes, but it is not going to bring the highest wisdom. You might be able to make ten million dollars, but it isn't going to bring the highest wisdom. I wouldn't trade any amount of money for that wisdom. It's not for sale, and it can't be bought or sold. Once it is recognized to be your own, it can never be taken away from you. Never.

HOW TO RELATE TO BODILY DEGENERATION

CHAPTER NINE

Through practice we learn to live as reality, along with its loud punctuations like degeneration, old age and death. Sudden illness, injury and pandemics are also loud punctuations. To live as the joyful, cheerful, spontaneous reality is the only recourse. None of these—sickness, old age and death—are actually spinning anyone out of spontaneous reality, because there is in fact *no individuality*. Individuality is a made-up dream. The sudden illness, the old age and the dying are all beneficial potency, and beneficial potency is found therein.

Some of us are older and already know what degeneration is. Actually, everyone is in the process of degenerating. One way to look at it is that it is present from the moment of birth onward—degeneration to death. Open intelligence itself is a great support, but in a Four Mainstays community we take great responsibility for ourselves and for the benefit of all. We can actually see when people are degenerating, and we have a sensitivity to that. We can step forward and offer assistance when that process is in place; we can carry their bag of groceries or open the car door or do whatever is needed.

When our data streams are running wild, it can be the case that what we care about is just ourselves—"number one," and that's all—and we cannot see anything else. The zenith of practice is to take in all the suffering of all beings in all worlds and to give to all beings and all worlds one's happiness and realization. This is the access to the mind of great bliss seeing emptiness. It is a very powerful practice and it does bring total relief, but it does take some daring as well!

This Teaching is not just a bunch of words that point to something far off and remote; rather, it is something that can be tested in your own experience, in which you find a power over all the pathologies you thought you had. All the pathological conditionings have been adopted, and just as easily they can be dispensed with. It's much easier to dispense with them than to hang on to them. Hanging on to them only brings decrease in energy while increasing fatigue and aging. When you simply settle in to the ease of what you actually are, it's wonderful and comfortable, and at the same time this easefulness may contradict everything you have ever believed about your reified self.

You eventually come to see that data pose no threat; whether it is good or bad, data pose no threat. Data are open intelligence itself—always on, always powerful, always clear. It may take a while to get the hang of it, but in the meantime, whatever thought, emotion, sensation or experience you're having, you can rely on open intelligence rather than emphasizing the data. This is the greatest healing act that will ever occur for you or for anyone else.

SKILLFUL AGING

In living a life based only on data, life is one disappointment after another, ending with the final disappointment of death. The final blow. The older you get, believe me, the more disappointments there are, and that is the way it is when life is based on data. If we can't go into old age, sickness and death completely relaxed, we're going to have a very hard time. No matter what we've accomplished earlier in life, it's going to be of little use to us when the body falls apart. Learned knowledge is of no comfort. The only thing that can guarantee you that you're not going to be overwhelmed by what occurs late in your life is to really be rooted in strong mind. That is the best medicine.

If you just sit here right now and start thinking about all the places in your body that don't feel right, you would be a mad man by the end of the day, and you would have a doctor's bill that no one could pay! This is another very good reason for the proper training in education in the nature of mind.

Because we have been trained that we're sinners or that we're bad people or that we have done so many wrong things in our lives, we tend to think of ourselves that way, and as a result when we are old, we have remorse and regret. But when we are no longer reifying our data, that is no longer the case, because it's known for certain that birth, life and death are not. They are not and they are not-not. This "not and not-not" is at first only an experience, but as we reflect on it, it becomes a deep understanding, and then we see we don't have to put it into a conceptual framework.

The reified notions we have learned about what's going on with us—our emotions, thoughts, sensations and other experience—is what's going to govern us during our lifetime unless we have basic knowledge. If we think that certain of our emotions are painful or bad, or certain thoughts are painful or bad, or bodily pains are painful or bad, that belief is going to govern us. If we can't bring basic knowledge to afflictive states, then afflictive states are going to rule our entire life, from the bookend of birth to the bookend of death. That's just the way it is.

These Teachings really are Teachings that are preparations for death, but they work during life, too! Of course, there's the life cycle: there's birth and early life and adulthood and then there's old age, degeneration and death. Spend one day thinking about that and it will be perfectly clear that a death teaching is necessary. People already know about the old age and death part, but the degeneration part is one that is maybe not considered as much, but which could be a very lengthy one to deal with.

It could start in earnest at any time in life. For instance, you could get Parkinson's disease in your twenties, and there would be a very, very long period of degeneration. We have been using this analogy of surfing the tsunami all through the book, but wow, what a tsunami of emotion would there be when you hear the words, "You have Parkinson's disease and you will not get better." In a crucial and challenging time like that, you definitely want to rely on what will most ably carry you through and which will empower you with the clarity and courage needed to deal with such an experience.

No one knows how long or what form degeneration in our own lives might take, but for everyone it will come at a certain point. When you're young, if you get sick, you go the doctor, you get fixed and you're ready to go again. Degeneration in old age means that you may go to the doctor and the doctor will say, "You will not be getting better." That's what degeneration means: you will not be getting better.

There are certain pains that almost everyone might feel in their lives more or less, according to their degree of sensitivity, and as one grows older these things increase. There are also different effects on one's lifestyle, such as the inability to sleep—maybe even for days. And then during the time of being unable to sleep, there may be rumination about the past with very few aspirations for the future. So, that's another possible part of old age, degeneration and death—no longer having aspirations for the future.

When you're young you're thinking ahead to what you're going to do next, but for some older people there is no aspiration in terms of the future. Many of the things that kept people feeling uplifted according to their data streams are completely gone, taken away. However, what need this matter in the short moment of the unimaginable, dimensionless, beginningless beginning and inexhaustible end? That's what a short moment introduces us to—beginningless and endless open intelligence, pristine and pure. A short moment is a skillful means of enjoying reality *as it is*.

As we get older a lot of our previous strategies won't work any longer. Maybe as a young person we could perform all sorts of incredible physical feats, but in a few years we won't be able to do that. A lot of the antidotes that we had used won't work anymore, and then we're just left with whatever is going on. It's really recommended that while we're young and strong to take advantage of the strength of youth to devote it to full-on, always-on strong mind. This way, if we happen to go through the process of degeneration and aging, we will be strong in the knowledge that aging, illness and death are simply data streams. We'll be able to shine with bliss, regardless of what is going on.

A lot of older people don't have an open forum for discussing what's going on. Some may be complaining much of the time, while others will be saying that everything is just fine, but often they don't have a deep understanding of what's going on or a way to find a remedy that's soothing for them. However, whatever age we are, we have a *choice* in each moment of how to be with what's going on.

With these Teachings, sickness, aging, degeneration and death are moments of incredible direct crossing and of breakthrough. They are moments of more and more shine, of an agency that had been unknown before—an intelligent agency that has a knowingness of itself as spontaneous reality. It has beneficial powers beyond compare. This means that whatever beneficial potency has been brought into being during this precious human

birth, the agency of that is greater and greater. It is ever increasing without any expanse of time.

As we age, for most of us there could be more and more symptoms of disease, both psychological and physical, and over the course of our life we learn to elaborate those in different ways. We learn to develop descriptive frameworks for them, and the context for all these descriptions is the *absence* of reliance on open intelligence. It is easy to get caught up in talking about psychological and physical symptoms, but is this the way we want to be greeting all these things?

When we focus solely on our symptoms, we might want to go out and form friendships with other people who are focusing on the same thing. We want someone to say, "How is that rheumatoid arthritis," or "How are your bowel issues doing?" When we focus on our symptomatology in a conversation, we are attracting that kind of response. We want someone to focus on psychological or physical symptoms along with us, and this helps support the belief that they are real. In gaining stability and confidence in awareness, we see that this emphasis on our physical and psychological symptoms can be brought to a complete stop. Strong mind is now the focus of our attention—and not our symptoms.

ZIJI RINPOCHE SHARES ABOUT HER OWN EXPERIENCE

If I look back just for a moment at any outcomes I expected or wanted for whatever philosophy, psychology, spirituality or religion I was involved in, and then I look at the way things are now, I never could have dreamt that such things would be possible! I can say that I live like the forever youthful sun, and I really mean it and do not burst out in sarcastic laughter when I say it! There is so much motivation and aspiration inspired in me to benefit myself, to benefit others and to be of great benefit to all. "The forever youthful sun" is a metaphor for the youthful

vitality and vigor that is a natural aspect of open intelligence, no matter how old and decrepit we are.

In my own age group I see a lot of the effects of degeneration, including in myself. With the future innovations in health care, there may be greater relief from the degeneration part, but there can never be any guarantees. There are always the sorts of things that can come along where the doctors just say, "We can't do anything about this." By practicing these Teachings, especially when you're young, they will bring you a life of total release during the process of old age, extended degeneration and death.

I can't really tell you how exactly it happened and what the steps were that brought me here today to sit in this chair to speak to you. I can't really measure that totally; however, I do know that at one time I was a very emotional person and also extremely intellectual. Not a good combination, because no matter what it was, I could think up a storm about it! But at some point, I had to cast all of that aside.

One of the things that allowed that to happen for me was aging— seeing my children age and myself aging, and as a result seeing what is important in life and what is not. I could see that it was very important for my sons' lives that they should have complete mental and emotional stability that came from the heart. I stayed with that for them, and I stayed with that for myself, and guess what? Positive result for them, positive result for mom.

One of the things I can say about getting older is that the older you become, the more you have bodily ailments and the more your friends have bodily ailments—at times very severe bodily ailments. The older we become, the more death affects us and the more we see it right before our eyes. We also see that what our teachers have been telling us—impermanence, old age, sickness and death—is true. These Teachings were all developed to support people on their deathbed—not so much living life, although it did support in living life, as we can all tell—but on their deathbed. As death teachings they weren't necessarily developed for enlightenment. It just so happens that enlightenment came rushing in!

When people get to be my age, they start kind of falling like flies. That's part of the impermanence of life. One thinks, "Oh, I'm so old; where am I going to live? I don't have a job now, so what am I going to do with myself? My kids won't take care of me. I don't have any money to go somewhere." Suffering, old age, sickness and death: impermanence. This is the reason that the teaching of impermanence is so very important.

When I was a young woman I met some very interesting women from Berkeley, California. They were all just turning sixty, and they were part of the radical lesbian movement, and many had left their husbands, changed their names, and taken on new lifestyles. One of them wrote a book called *Over the Hill*, in which she described the experience of being a woman who is aging and becoming increasingly invisible to all the attention with which she had identified herself when she was a younger woman.

Many of us gather our sense of identification by the attention that other people pay to us, and we may be wrapped up in sexual attention. "Am I sexually attractive to this one or that one?" These thoughts occur even if we have no plans whatsoever of ever having any kind of erotic intercourse with them. However it may have been for us, open intelligence is where it's at. Everything that's looked for in all these desires—self-worth, confidence, happiness, fulfillment—is already present in the indivisibility of perfect, indestructible open intelligence and whatever is appearing. Through this, one has a very clear knowledge of what to do and how to act with everyone.

When I was young and I would think about my old age, I thought, "Gee, someday I'm going to be old and decrepit. I see it happening all around me, so I know it's going to happen to me too. What am I going to do then?" I could picture myself sitting in a chair with a cocktail, but it didn't turn out that way! The old and decrepit part did, but I wasn't counting on the forever youthful sun as an outcome! Open intelligence's beneficial potencies are full of surprises, full of inconceivable utterances of every kind—of the thought variety, of the emotional variety and with all kinds of sensations that could never be conceived through conventional conceptual frameworks.

If we settle for conventional conceptual frameworks, then we miss all these incredible things. Then we only get the "old and decrepit" part, when in fact there are so many amazing things just being poured onto us. The reality of who we are is that we are bliss-born; we are born to be blissful, dynamically bright and intelligent. We're born to solve problems that have defied solution. We are the only creature that we know of that is born with the knowledge of the entire universe within us and the power to use that in a beneficial way.

THE BEST MEDICINE

CHAPTER TEN

You may have one of those containers where the medicines you take are all collected according to the day of the week, but the best medicine you can have is not in any of those containers. The best medicine is the basic knowledge of open intelligence. That's what you really want to have when you get old—or at any other time in life.

The practice of short moments is a distinct world of complete relaxation. All the spas and other places that are supposed to help you relax when you are older and sicker, well, the primordial spa is always available! The primordial spa of complete relaxation comforts all, it doesn't matter what the experience is.

By the power of open intelligence, you get to see who you really are, and through the practice of short moments the growing familiarity with open intelligence is always opening up more and more. It doesn't go in reverse; you're always learning more about who you are. You're always feeling more empowered, no matter what your situation, even if you're really sick or dying. When you get sick, the thoughts may come, "Oh dear, this is so miserable and horrible. Dying is going to be a bummer, and no one will want to be around me."

By the power of open intelligence, you're able to flow along with everything. It doesn't matter what it is, you know that you're going to be okay—whether it's life or death or any other data stream that comes along. Whatever your age, everything rests unavoidably in open intelligence. Nothing can ever be removed from open intelligence. There's no concept or circumstance you can come up with that's ever going to destroy open intelligence or take you out of the indestructible family of open intelligence.

If you live a life wrapped in ordinary reified activities, holding those to be the only reality, it's like living with your head in the mouth of a crocodile. It really is. It can't sustain you over the short term and it can't sustain you over the long term either. But by gaining confidence in strong mind, you surround yourself with loving open intelligence and the wisdom, clarity and insight that are natural aspects of it.

In relying on open intelligence, you are never alone, no matter where you are. Even if you are physically alone, you are never alone. You are never separate from the complete relief of open intelligence, the relationship that will never let you down, the way of being that is completely unchanging, that can't be modified or altered or taken away.

This is what you really want to gain confidence in, and not something else. Everything will be destroyed, no matter what it is. You want to gain confidence in that which will never be destroyed. That which will never be destroyed is the basic state—loving open intelligence. That's your primary identity, always has been, always will be. To believe anything else is to believe in falsehood.

Do you know what is really the greatest pandemic of our time? It is the pervasive, worldwide ignorance of open intelligence. The mental illness of ignorance divides people against one another and divides people within themselves. Our most basic right is sanity. We need to know what sanity is and that the most pervasive health problem is to lack basic sanity. It is extremely important to know that this insanity—this lack of knowledge of open intelligence—is a pandemic and that human society is in denial about this pandemic. It actually is an illness of mind, speech, body, qualities and activities. Why? Because unless we have an introduction to basic sanity, we never know what our strengths, gifts and talents to be of benefit to all are, and we might never meet anyone who can point that out to us.

FLEETING AND IMPERMANENT

Often when people have afflictive emotions, they want to just be free of them, and they may try to somehow disarm the afflictive data and make them go away, or least to neutralize them. However, to only neutralize data is actually quite harmful, because the afflictive data have not really been dealt with skillfully, but have only been hidden or postponed. If something is merely neutralized, when a very big issue that is unexpected comes along—like a sudden illness, a death in the family, a severe car accident—all the data streams that were there before the neutralization are back again in full force, or even in greater force. Please don't think that neutralization is something that will actually work, because it doesn't; it doesn't work at all.

We may have been groping for all kinds of antidotes that have never really worked, but it's only because we didn't know how to resolve the constant labeling of everything. It's really important to examine labels to know what they are, and to know that there isn't any label that has any kind of power or influence over well-being. Death can be experienced as blissful, and old age and sickness can be experienced in the same way, but only if one instinctively recognizes the basic state.

Things in life are fleeting; they are completely impermanent and will never last. They are just spontaneous appearances. Place all of your "effort" in what is effortless. This is what you really want to do. This is the course of action you want to take for your precious life. Distraction by all kinds of other things and seeing them as important will never lead anywhere. When you get old, sick and infirm, which most people will eventually be, how are all these distracting activities going to support you? Are they going to give you complete relief? Are they going to be there for you when you are old and alone? When surfing tsunamis like these, what is it that will carry you through in all ways?

We must face the fact of disease, old age and death, as well as the fact that death can come at any moment. Yes, death can come at any moment, and so it's really interesting that it's only upon complete acceptance of illness, old age and death that arrogance is outshone, because until then we may have some kind of subtle irrational idea that we as the body are somehow immortal. It's very humbling to know that the body will die. When we totally realize the true meaning of sickness, old age and death, and are prepared for death, then we will no longer suffer from this kind of arrogance and pride.

With greater confidence in open intelligence, there is no more caving in to the belief that death is the end of life. We have been taught that things like illness, aging and the degeneration of the body are all harbingers of this thing called death, but at the same time secretly we may have this subtle but unspoken notion that, "Everyone else is going to die, but not me." When we have this kind of attitude, it's very difficult for us to be around people who are dying or to think of ourselves dying.

But in the pure feed of radical reality and in living as that reality itself, we recognize that life, birth, death, waking, dreaming, sleeping are all subsumed in open intelligence, and we realize that death is just another data stream. The all-creating essence is always in command; it never goes anywhere. Whatever it shines forth might be called all kinds of things, but so what?

In this Teaching we go to any length to help people see that there is another way to be—one that does not involve ravaging ourselves with constant data streams of suffering, and becoming more and more immersed in a limited sense of self as we go into sickness, degeneration and death. Very often in this culture of isolation and primitiveness we feel completely alone and isolated in our emotions, our thoughts, our sensations of the body or our experiences.

The way to think of any issue is in terms of "How can this situation be one that is for the benefit of all?" That's how I relate to any of my bodily disintegrations. There is nothing to do. We can just relax, and if we need support we can always ask for it. Taking in all the world's suffering in relation to our own dismay of the moment, whatever that might be, and then realizing there are so many with exactly the same experience in that moment is the beginning of spontaneous self-release.

If we have not learned about open intelligence when we go through the process of degeneration and death, that process can be very painful. I know some people who live in senior facilities, and they said that their hardest time is at night when they can't sleep. So many of them have insomnia, and they lie awake and think about the past. They think about the bad things that happened in the past, and they just can't stop that train from running through their minds. Then they are told about short moments and they take to the practice, and it is an opening to no longer needing to focus on oneself, one's insomnia and one's regrets. What a relief. Yes, that is a big relief indeed.

I had a very good friend who had taught at the University of California at Berkeley and who had published many books. He ended up having Alzheimer's disease in his nineties and didn't recognize anyone. He was at a place for people with dementia, but one of the things he could remember was the Serenity Prayer. "Grant me the serenity to accept things I cannot change, to change the things I can, and the wisdom to know the difference." It's a very beautiful way to be. Some of this—old age, dementia, mental and physical decline—sounds kind of scary, but this is where freedom in immediate perception comes in. By living our life such that we face every data stream, whatever it is, with a short moment of open intelligence, we will also be able to face the whole process of dementia and death.

In ancient times this Teaching was developed for people for when they had to face old age, sickness and death. I'll speak for myself as someone for whom these things are present in my life. Old age and sickness, yeah, I can attest to that. And then death, well, when I was young maybe I kind of thought I would never die, but death is something I am seeing more now. It's an actual part of the lives of many people I know that death from natural causes is just around the corner.

For some of you who are reading this, death may be just around the corner—not like tomorrow or the next day, but sometime soon. Without reliance on open intelligence, whatever comes to us will be bitter. It will leave a bitter taste in our mouth because we will know that we left what could have given us happiness.

Yet, you practitioners are happy, and you can understand that it's okay to get old. You're going to be fine. You're going to be more than fine because you will be relying on open intelligence. It is the sole panacea. It's the cure-all. You're not going to need anything else to make you happy.

We are so lucky. By practicing open intelligence for short moments, equalizing wisdom is there in all of these life passages. And again, it is *quantity* and not quality of short moments that matters. We have no idea what the quality is, because it changes according to time, place and circumstance, so quantity is what's important. Quantity is what leads to always-on obvious open intelligence.

In living in exaltation, it doesn't matter whether we're sick or degenerating or dying or if we have gray hair or young hair; we're so happy to have shed the suit of anxiety.

To have colds and flu when you are young is good practice for old age, sickness and death. With the cold and the flu, it is good to not get caught up in the data streams, but to rest. To rest as open intelligence is so profound when we aren't feeling well, because it can allow us to see that the illness is a data stream. Then we won't be so involved in the data stream that we might not even be aware of anyone else around us. We will be able to be open to the people around us, care about them and be concerned about how they are.

Physical ailments tend to get worse over time, not better. Having the flu in your twenties will just be kind of a bother, but a bother you can definitely deal with. With the thirties and forties, it starts to get a little bit more annoying. But what you have for a few days when you are younger, in your sixties you might have it for two or three weeks. In the seventies, eighties and nineties, well, it can take you out.

The sixties are like a bridge of no return. You see clearly there is no return; you're not going back. The hopes and dreams you had when you were younger are no longer possible. There is no future of a career or children or that kind of thing. Some of you who are young have parents who are in their sixties, and even though they may not say these things to you, you can be sure that these things are coming up for them. So, it's a wonderful time for compassion and reaching out.

If your thinking goes off on some bizarre line of thought, the golden key is always turned on. You know exactly who you are, and "the thinker" ain't it! Just let the thinker do whatever it will. Pretty soon the body starts doing whatever it will, and there may be nothing that you can do about it. No matter how powerful you think you are to stop death, there's nothing you can do about it.

The point of this is that many here are young and many are older, but whatever your age, death will come to you in some way. Either young or old, by accident or illness or some other means, death will certainly come. Through the power of bliss-benefit potency, you see the reality of what your mind and body actually are. You see that your reality is the reverberation of the sound of all sound. When you know this, then you really know who you are.

We can reflect on and plan for our death and what it might be like, and what it might be like to not have a body any longer— but to still have open intelligence. At the point of death, there may be all kinds of images appearing and many different sounds heard, along with all kinds of other things—things never before seen, never before heard. We will definitely want to be able to rest and to stay with open intelligence.

For those who had a Guru, the ancient teachings taught that the dying person should imagine the Guru on the top of the head. Even though we won't have a body any longer, it takes a while to adjust to that, hence the instruction to imagine the Guru on the top of the head.

The Guru doesn't need to be physically present to be giving foremost instructions. In an unexpected situation, like being very sick and in the emergency room, the best thing for the student to do is to think about the Guru. It really is the best thing to do, because one can merge with the luminosity. One comes to see that one is non-different from the Guru, and to reveal that is the Guru's job description! The job description isn't to show how they are better than we are. It's to show the equalness and evenness of who we are.

Whether sick or suffering, victim to robbery or theft, insulted, slandered, emotionally or physically abused, in adversity or hunger or whatever your experience, don't become despondent, depressed and anxious. Remain cheerful, inspired and in good spirits, resting as the sublime essence of these countless data descriptions.

EXAMPLES AND DEMONSTRATIONS

One of the concerns I've seen come up for some people is the fact that they are getting wrinkles and gray hair as they age. The wrinkles and gray hair are actually a helpful reminder that old age, sickness and death are getting closer and closer, so now is the time for us to do some heavy duty resting! This disposition also really helps us to be with our friends who are aging and sick. It isn't any longer all about just ourselves; our resting is indivisible, so we are indivisibly reaching out to everyone.

I have an older friend here in town who used to take care of our dogs. I would take the dogs to her and she would look at me and she would say, "You really look beautiful. But just wait, in about ten years you'll start to fall apart!" But I feel forever youthful, so I don't have any notion of needing any of that—the beauty or the youth—to keep things real.

In the last years I've had some major health issues, and my husband has been there for me one hundred percent. But I do know some married people where one of them gets sick with something that they're not going to recover from, and then the other one leaves. Conventional logic and reason look at things in one way, but insight and discernment come from sublime wisdom, so they have an entirely different way of looking.

I know a thriving young person who suddenly was very sick. The doctors and nurses had come in to tell him what was wrong, and he just said, "Oh, thank you very much for letting me know and thank you so much for helping me," and the doctors and nurses were touched and they replied, "Oh, you don't need to thank us!" The patient said, "I'm really grateful that you're here to take care of me, and I thank you from my heart. I so appreciate all that you have done for me." Well, that sort of patient will always be remembered, because they have plowed the fields of emptiness and they have harvested the joyous glow of indivisibility. See? Emptiness is the joyous glow of indivisibility.

I can see in myself that the body disintegrates in aging, and I've also seen my Guru Wangdor Rimpoche go through glaucoma, cataract surgery and knee surgery. Before his knee surgery he couldn't go up to the cave where he stayed because his legs wouldn't take him up there anymore. He did have a beautiful room inside a big statue of Padmasambhava, but he wanted to be in his cave. For a while he was sitting in his bed in the statue, and although he didn't necessarily prefer it, he was shining nevertheless. He wasn't feeling or taking in grumpiness at all; his only reality was pure transmission. This is a very great example, because we know that also earlier in his life Wangdor Rimpoche was faced with many different kinds of things, but what did he choose? He chose Bodhicitta.

AT DEATH, GREAT BLISS SEEING EMPTINESS

CHAPTER ELEVEN

Many of us here are young, but I can guarantee you that what the teachings say about old age, sickness and death is absolutely true. Those of us who do not die prematurely will experience old age, sickness and death. No matter how much we exercise now or how good our nutrition is or whatever other means we might take, anyone who lives long enough will go through old age, sickness and death.

The reason that this is emphasized is that when people die, they tend to have all kinds of negative points of view, and that could be true for any of us. We could also die of some horrid disease; but what is going to support us in that? Will it be the drugs and doctors alone? Well, they might help us. However, having received this precious instruction about resting naturally in the midst of dilemma, we want to be resting naturally with the horrid disease as well.

These days, not only are the old getting ill, but people of all ages are becoming deathly ill from the virus—from young people all the way through to the very old. I suggest thinking about death and thinking about old age. Reflect on old age, sickness and death—reflect on this. The deterioration of the body will come; it could come when you're still young, but definitely when you are older. We never know when death will come, so it's essential to prepare for it now.

Reflecting on death and being available for people who are dying is a big part of my practice. Everyone here has witnessed death in some form, and right now one could say that we have a pandemic of death; that's what we have. Do not be afraid. Rely on open intelligence rather than on the data. We want to be vigilant. We want to take the best care of our precious human bodies that we possibly can, and we can perhaps make old age a little better for ourselves and for others by being open, just simply open to what's going on.

When we die, we can't take anything with us. This is the final reminder that everything is impermanent. We can't take our body or any of our accomplishments with us, or our money, our friends or family. No one goes with us. Everyone will die, and we could die this instant. We never know. One of the primary reasons—in fact some teachers say the *only* reason they teach—is to prepare people for the moment of death. When we die, great bliss seeing emptiness never changes. The mind is still active, even though we're shedding the body. Right after we die, there is a flash of clear light, and in recognizing strong mind, we are free in that instant.

It's so difficult for many people to face the reality of death, but we all must face that reality. The more we have lived as open intelligence, the more we will see that death is another data stream and that open intelligence never dies. It is indestructible, completely indestructible, and when we hear words like "heaven," that is what that word means—open intelligence that is indestructible. Open intelligence is very powerful, very, very powerful. It places us wherever we want to be; however, if we don't know about it, we can end up in all kinds of places we don't want to be. So, to know intelligence and to stay put as open intelligence, this is where it's at!

Birth, life, death, waking, dreaming, sleeping, all of these are the force-field of beneficial potency. I know that many of you already know that death is but a passing fancy, and that recognition will fully carry you through when the tsunami of emotions comes at the point of death. Death is just another step on the trip, the inexhaustible, forever trip, the forever and always reality that is *as it is*.

Death is like a dream. Just like all the rest of this, it's like a dream. In the blink of an eye, it's a dream. Sleeping at night, it's a dream. Dreaming at night, it's a dream. The waking state itself—like a dream. All like a dream. We live as the bold brightness in which death is just another series of data streams.

What appearance could be more demanding of us than death? Death is inevitable, and no one is left unaffected. A fundamental human dilemma is that throughout all of our life we know we will eventually die. In acknowledging this universal condition, we develop great sensitivity and compassion for ourselves and for everyone else, because we know that *everyone* dies and not just us.

For me it's important to consider the reality that death can come at any moment, so no matter what our next action is, it can be filled with bravery and courage. If there is a feeling about a challenge we have, "Oh, I won't be able to accomplish that,"

another thought could be, "I might die in two seconds, so why don't I spend the next seconds as an expression of total courage?"

The obsessive-compulsive focus on the body and its goings-on is mental illness. Living a life with complete ignorance of brightly glowing great illumination as the only reality of all is mental illness. Mortality is a fantasy. We need to realize that we live as the great illumination of inexhaustible agency, the inexhaustible capacity to glow brighter and brighter.

What we call death is secret living energy. After death of the body our agency of glittering brightness reshapes—or not. If we have been told that what happens at death is decided for us by great institutions or traditions, it must be seen that this is completely false. Through a life of spontaneous devotion, we instinctively realize more and more that it's up to us. What we want at death— who we are and where we go—is up to us. As we come closer and closer to death, whose time is never known, we realize more and more exactly what it is we want at death.

Because we have been told that we are original sinners and such "bad" people, we think that we need to do a lot of good things in order to escape all of the things that possibly could happen at death. However, now we are learning that we are actually living energy constantly birthing, birthing, birthing, and that for us there is no death. There is no death; there is only birthing, birthing, birthing. Maybe some of us have already realized that, and it's very clear to us that this is the way it is and that we're not living for death, death, death. Live for birth, live for birth, live for birth, constant birthing.

AT ANY INSTANT

Death could come at any instant, that's the reality. If we're looking for reality, that's our reality as human beings. From the moment we're born, death could come at any instant. We need to have this foremost in our mind all the time. It's really a great idea to think about death. We're here right now, but an instant from now we could all be gone. This recognition clears the way for deep understanding.

Brilliant, knowing emptiness brings complete ease and beneficial potency, including at death. Death is just this—empty-beauty-knowing, empty-beauty-seeing. That's it. No different from any other flash instant. Why make a big deal out of it? That's it, just this.

We don't know whether we will die as an individual or in the context of the deaths of many people all at once, or maybe our pocket of the multiverse might be suddenly sucked into oblivion. We never know. What we can count on is that we remain exactly as we are. If we live life terrified and afraid, constantly trying to hold onto our self-identity, then what will happen at death? Exactly the same thing we've trained up in all along: terror, fear, trying to hold onto self-identity, not wanting to let go of that form of meat! Why hang onto that idea at the moment of death?

DEATH AS AN EASYGOING AND CAREFREE MOMENT

We should know in a profound way that birth, life and death are all timelessly free appearances of a more fundamental condition. When we become familiar with the reality that all the appearances, including death, are wide-open and have never been made into anything with an independent nature, then when death comes, we are ready, and that enormous wave can be surfed with ease. Death can then be an easygoing and carefree moment that is complete and identical to any other moment.

When we gain familiarity with open intelligence, we have nothing to fear; even a terminal illness won't be daunting for us. We're able to be without impediment, whatever the situation is. This increasing familiarity with open intelligence will carry us through all the doctor's appointments, all the worries about the changes in our lives because of sickness and aging, and all the concerns about dying.

The attitude we have towards death either gives us freedom in our life or lack of freedom. If we have the idea that death is the end of us, then we'll consider death to be an enemy, and it will be something that we're scared to death of! We won't want it to happen, because we think it means the end; but thinking that death is the end is just an inherited assumption about the way things are.

Usually scary thoughts are associated with death. When scary thoughts of illness or death come up, take a short moment over and over again as the thoughts arise, and just know then that you are resting as the inexhaustibility of pure illumination, of clear-light seeing and loving. This is exactly who you are, always have been, are now and will always be. This is the truth of it.

The Choice at Death

When we realize open intelligence's perfect love, then we know what our body really is. At death we have that choice; we can check that box on the application form of "open intelligence's perfect love, perfect capability and perfect knowledge."

At death all kinds of things come up for everyone. There are thoughts and experiences, emotions and sensations never had before. It's just like taking a trip to an unknown place. If you take a trip somewhere you've never been before, there's probably some anxiety about it and wondering what it's going to be like there. At death we are leaving the human body aside from our realm of experience, which means that we are open intelligence only, and that is all that is obvious to us.

At death, whatever we think of, there we are. If we think of anxiety, immediately we are in the most anxious atmosphere. If we are afraid and we think we're going to go to hell because we've been bad, that is exactly where we will immediately be, because there's nothing in the way of anything. If we think of a heaven realm, then we'll be there too.

But is that what we really want? There are other opportunities available as well. Open intelligence is the brightness of great benefit, and the brightness of great benefit pervades everything, including all of these realms just mentioned. It is a choice, just like in life it is a choice. No matter what anyone says to the contrary, this choice is definitive; it is the case. This is not just something that I'm making up, but something that has been the case and is the case for countless beings already.

For most people it is only at death that they recognize the reality of their identity as beneficial potency. Because they have no experience of beneficial potency in life, that experience at death is fleeting, so they don't know it is their reality. Instead of just resting as that, they go on to follow all the mixed-up neurochemical states as the brain dies off, one part after another, while everything goes wild and experiences are beyond any dreams we have ever had.

No positive psychology is going to help that, I can guarantee you. Only knowing that everything is pure benefit magic can help. This knowing is so deep that it fills the vast expanse inexhaustibly in all cardinal directions and beyond, subsuming everything in its utter simplicity, in its utter reality and in its utter identity as the identity of all.

When we're in the process of dying, the thoughts and emotions radically alter. One of the things that will happen is that the different sensory mechanisms of our body will shut down. The eyesight, the ability to feel tactile sensations, the ability to smell things or to hear or respond to what's being said—all of these will go one by one. Finally, the breathing and the heartbeat will also stop. We may have thoughts and emotions like, "I have eaten my last meal; I will never see my loved ones again; I am going somewhere and no one is going with me!"

If throughout our lives we've been indulging, renouncing or replacing our data in order to feel better, then at death we won't have the mental energy to do those things any longer. Our supposed ability to think our way into well-being or control our thoughts will also be lost. Unless we've learned to rely on open intelligence, none of the strategies we've cultivated during our lifetime for handling disturbing thoughts and emotions will help us when we die.

There are many powerful thoughts, emotions and experiences we'll have at death, and it's quite possible that they'll be far more afflictive than anything we've ever experienced before. But if we are relying on open intelligence, it's likely we'll be able to let these things be as they are. We're only distracted when we think something needs to be done about what's appearing. We can let all the thoughts, emotions and sensations that appear at death be as they are. Any thought or emotion will disappear in and of itself, like a line drawn in water. The appearances have no power whatsoever to affect us, unless we let them.

NO DEATH AT DEATH

Even though we will all die someday, it isn't the basic state that dies. Our phenomenal appearance may change, but it only changes into the continuous flow of the basic state—what it has always been anyway. When we recognize that the indestructible basic state is the basis of all of our appearances, including our death, then we can have an easeful death, because we're not looking at our death as being a separation or an end. We don't see it as something along the lines of, "I've had this life, and now I'm dead."

To acknowledge death in no way declares that open intelligence or the beneficial energy of open intelligence dies. The whole process of dying is the beneficial energy of open intelligence. When we take advantage of realizing open intelligence during our lifetime, at the moment of death we see that the transition is easy. In a way death is like changing careers, and being a human has been our career for a while. If we really take advantage of resting as and relying on open intelligence, we will be able to see death as a career change! It is a career change of furthering in another way the beneficial energy and perfect knowledge of open intelligence.

Those who lack education in the spontaneous commitment of open intelligence's beneficial potency and who observe contrived commitments of other lifestyles find it very difficult in each moment, and especially at death, to discover the innermost meaning. When we live as open intelligence's beneficial potency in every moment, we discover the innermost and most profound meaning of that moment. Our practical experience of living as that then prepares us for death and allows us to discover the innermost meaning of each moment at death.

Without the prior education, we have no preparation for the innermost meaning of death, which is that death is just another data stream in open intelligence. Being human is only one iteration of open intelligence's beneficial potency. Death is not the end of open intelligence. Open intelligence has no beginning, middle or end; it has no birth, life and death. The death of the human entity is a presentation of open intelligence. It is a celebration of the growth and expansion of pure transmission of open intelligence. Here we have the innermost meaning of open intelligence in every moment of life.

We really don't know exactly what will happen after the point of our death as a human agent. However, we do know that agency is inexhaustible. Reality is always on; it doesn't stop when we die. Reality doesn't go away when we die, and we don't go away when we die either; it's just that we rearrange the marbles we're playing with! The more trained up we are in open intelligence, the less fearful we are of death, the more in control we are of what happens after death, and the more we have some input in that whole situation.

SUPPORT AT DEATH

How can we support a family member in the process of degeneration and death who is not involved in the Teachings? Well, I've had an opportunity to participate in such a way in my own family, and I would simply state to the dying person, "Go to the light!" Go to the light, because clear light is the first experience upon death, and anyone can choose clear light at that point. However, if one hasn't been introduced, then usually they don't see the clear light or they don't recognize it. But if we can say to them, "Go to the light," that's the greatest support.

In Tibetan culture, those who have taken up this Teaching believe that everyone sees light when they die; without exception, everyone sees light. Some people know nothing about what it means to see light, but for people who know what it means to see light, they stay put in that light. When beings stay put in light, none of the other distractions come along. That is the best outcome.

We can be on our deathbed, but nothing changes the stainless space of who we are. When the body is shut down and the mind and speech are gone completely, primordial benefit is totally at ease. The best way to help a person who is suddenly seized by the death call is to read them a text from the Teaching, like *Pure Space,* or one of the beautiful texts on death. This will bring comfort to everyone involved. Otherwise, there is just pandemonium and complete panic and wondering what to do next. However, in the solidity of who we are, we can face anything, and we can face it in a completely relaxed manner.

A question might arise, "What will happen to me if I'm *not* prepared for death?" Well, the Dzogchen Teachings have an answer for that, and it is that if you hear *one* Dzogchen Teaching in your life, you will be prepared for death. It's a "good outcome," as we would say these days, a good outcome. What that means is that there's enough transmission passed on in one introduction to Dzogchen, so that in the death process one can say, "Oh wow, yes, I remember that. I heard about this, and right now I'm okay."

At one time early on in this Teaching there was a participant who was diagnosed with cancer. This was something unfamiliar and unexpected for everyone involved, but we were able to be completely together in that circumstance, serving completely, beneficially and entirely. Because we could serve like that, the participant did not have a death surrounded only by people that they had never seen before. There was in those last stages the immediacy of open intelligence for the person, and there was another participant who was there with them at their time of death reading *Pure Space*.

The dying person could relax into the reality of what they really are, rather than having all of the mystifying notions about death coming in like a tornado. The Teachings are very important lifestyle teachings. This way is the way of rest and the way of complete relaxation that opens up to us an adventure we never could have imagined.

There was once a very great master who was teaching, among other things, that one had to leave the world, live in a cave and sit in meditative absorption for many years in order to realize the ultimate. At some point, though, he said to himself, "No, this isn't it." This great man saw that the ultimate was not something to be acquired, but something that was ever-present, and that there was no destination and no one going there. He was able to go far beyond what he had previously taught, and he escaped from the cage of his philosophy.

As he was dying, he was completely at ease, and he was able to declare, "My delight in death is far, far greater than the delight of traders at making vast fortunes or those who are proud of their victory in battle or of those sages who have entered the rapture of perfect absorption. So, just as a traveller who sets out on the road when it is time, I will not remain in this world any longer, but will go to dwell in the stronghold of the great bliss of deathlessness."

Third Section

BODHICITTA, TONGLEN, DZOGCHEN, THE LINEAGE, THE GURU

BODHICITTA AND
THE ENLIGHTENMENT OF ALL

CHAPTER TWELVE

Inseparable from the self-perfected qualities and activities of beneficial potency is the passionate desire to benefit all. The best word for that is *Bodhicitta*—the deep desire in one's life to spontaneously benefit all. The strong desire of Bodhicitta rooted in compassion is to attain enlightenment in order to benefit all living beings. Any love of self that would lead to practicing open intelligence would also lead eventually to wanting open intelligence for all—first recognizing that everyone already *has* and *is* open intelligence, and then realizing that the enlightenment of all is one's goal in life. This is the way to benefit beings conclusively.

Open intelligence is the expression of love. It's so important to know that the Bodhicitta aspect is inseparable from open intelligence. There can be no true open intelligence without true Bodhicitta. When the term "open intelligence" is used, it automatically includes Bodhicitta.

Ordinary or relative Bodhicitta is about conceptually engendering compassionate activity in everyday life, so in that case there is only *conceptualized* practice. Whereas, ultimate Bodhicitta is enlightened qualities and enlightened energy, spontaneously present and responsive in all appearances. It's particularly dedicated to the enlightenment of all, and not just in a vague way. It is right now—enlightenment of all right now.

Why should it not be so? As enlightenment is present already and pervading everyone, why not enlightenment of all right now? It is a capacity of human life that has generally been ignored; yet, it is acknowledged in some respects. Whether it's spoken of as oneness with God, oneness with Jesus, oneness with the Holy Spirit, oneness with the unspeakable or unspoken or whatever it might be, all of these point to some kind of realization. However, it's in the *actual experience* that they actually come forth.

Just as one understands the difference between wishing to go on a journey and actually setting out upon the journey, the wise should also recognize the difference. Bodhicitta in aspiration brings about great results, even as we continue to circle within negativity; yet, it does not bring about a ceaseless stream of benefit, for that will come solely from *active* Bodhicitta. From the moment we genuinely take up the irreversible attitude of open intelligence, we aspire to liberate beings entirely. Wanting realization, we spontaneously want the benefit of all beings, even though this intention may not be obvious to us at first.

THE SKILLFUL MEANS OF LOVING BODHICITTA

Self-contempt is so pervasive in so many cultures around the world. There are very few people who are free of this, so it is something that is shared by so very many, and all who break free need to take a clear look at self-contempt. To see clearly, "Wow, for all these years loathing of myself has so much been a part of my experience," is an act of compassion. Think of all the people in the world who are plagued by self-contempt due to the culture's reification of who they are.

When you rest for a short moment, the energy of the Lineage is bearing fruit, and soon the self-contempt goes. You may continue to feel self-contemptuous in certain specific ways, but in that, to just rest and see yourself as you really are brings about deep understanding. You see how self-contempt has played itself out for you, and you take responsibility. It's an act of taking responsibility in your practice. It is a form of Bodhicitta towards oneself.

One of the hindrances to realization is feeling that we don't deserve enlightened energy or that we're too unworthy or we've done too many questionable things to ever have enlightened energy. These feelings are normal, so, it's all fine. At the same time, it is important to see that to have any kind of thought or feeling—no matter how negative it might be—is just more fuel for realization, *because that thought is nothing other than open intelligence itself*!

It's important to uphold everything that is occurring in an all-inclusive way. It is absolutely essential to the full realization of Bodhicitta to see all of the occurrences of any situation through the eyes of pure perception. This is the only possibility whatsoever of recognizing sublime wisdom. The "surfing of the tsunami" that we have been speaking of in this book is always in the context of this pure perception, this sublime wisdom, and it is this that will carry you through.

These are very important instructions, and while they are simple, sometimes they aren't easy. So, what I recommend is, do your best and be your best with motivation and intention. Don't put yourself down; don't put yourself down or put yourself up—

either of those. "Putting yourself down" and "putting yourself up" are both self-aggression, but open intelligence is present in both "putting yourself down" and "putting yourself up." Be as you are, be as you are. In whichever way we have learned to describe the dynamic energy of data, simply *be*! By this practice, the reification is realized to be the sublime energy of wisdom and compassion. In the context of our reified life, we didn't know that data are the sublime energy of wisdom and compassion, so we created an entire world out of the data. We just made a mistake, that's all.

To me Bodhicitta is like the lotus, an exquisite flower appearing out of the mud and opening up with not a trace of mud on it. I don't use this traditional metaphor very often because I don't see any mud anywhere, so to me it's more like finally noticing sunlight in the sky. Sunlight and the sky are inseparable, and this is what Bodhicitta offers—inseparability. We do this by taking in the suffering of anything at all—a bird, a tree withering away and dying, a person who is suffering or a planet unable to any longer uphold its ability to thrive—and giving out all of our beneficial intent.

When we get up in the morning and reflect on emptiness, our primary intention within that can be Bodhicitta. It doesn't matter whether we're cooking, gardening or sitting in meditation, the superior intention is to benefit all. One takes all of one's strengths, gifts and talents and offers them to lessen the suffering of others. The greatest suffering is in not being enlightened, or stated in another way, in not being enlightenment. It can be termed "being enlightenment" or "not being enlightenment"

because there is no person who "has" enlightenment. "To not be enlightenment" is the greatest suffering.

If we really take a look and reflect on our daily circumstance, we can see that each instant is like a rainbow in the sky, in that a rainbow in the sky is always changing. It's always changing, and it eventually resolves into basic space. So, for each of us this is true; each instant is like a rainbow in the sky. We can't really tie it together to a past or to a future; it's only here, right now. Through this simple meditation we are able to outshine our reification of data. Then in the end, reification itself is also outshone, and there is the grandeur of the mind of great bliss seeing emptiness—full-hearted Bodhicitta, compassion, unexcelled wisdom and sublime enlightened energy.

In terms of finding something that would lead to stability in life, the only thing that I found that really worked was love, so that is what I practiced. Not make-believe love, but the love that we all are, and resting as that for short moments, many times. With that I was able to see clearly the things that had no chance of providing ultimate happiness, like money or relationships. There's no way to count on money or relationships to provide happiness. It may be that as a byproduct of your own practice you have a good relationship, but true happiness will not come from the relationship itself. No one is going to love us enough or make us happy enough to feel happy and loved totally and forever.

What I think about when I come to know that a person has a very difficult situation is, "What is it that could bring complete relief to this situation and to this person?" And I pray—with my definition of prayer—I pray that that person can have a very strong spark of life, and the taste, beauty and the brightness of what that is. If they are gravely ill or even dying, I pray that their sickness or their dying can be that brightness, rather than fear and struggle.

Much earlier, when I was younger, often I couldn't sleep. I would be in bed, but I would imagine myself walking up and down the streets in the little town where I live. I knew everyone who lived in each of the houses, and so I would visualize walking by their house with them in there, and then I would say a little prayer, then go on to the next house and say a prayer. Because I could so often not get to sleep, I walked through the whole town many times in my mind!

When we had 9/11 and the Twin Towers were hit by the airplanes, everyone in my town was frantic. There were jets flying up and down the coast to protect the United States from invasion, so it was pretty stark. People didn't know what to do; everyone was so panicked and anxious. I didn't know what to do either, so I baked a lot of cookies and took them around and gave the cookies to everyone I would see. This is just an example of what might pop up to respond to a time of panic.

If we only have a contrived idea of compassion, it may be that we think that the situation needs to look a certain way, such as, "Oh yes, in this situation we're all going to meditate." Well, that might be good for a few people, and meditating can certainly go along with passing out the cookies—as the "cookie meditation" is part of meditating!—but, rather than holding to fixed ideas about how things should be, we can be open to what might spontaneously emerge in response to an unexpected situation.

I am giving you some examples just so you have some idea from another person—some things I've done—rather than just talking about these things abstractly. I do know from my own experience that in terms of uncontrived compassion, all kinds of incredible ideas can come about that we didn't read about in a book or we didn't have to manufacture in some way. They just appear spontaneously.

THE GENEROSITY OF BODHICITTA

I became convinced that, through being devoted to the benefit of all, this would be the way to accomplish the things I wanted to accomplish. I want to encourage you never to step away from your ideals, because even though you may have periods where you don't feel like it makes a difference or you don't know whether you can go on, if you keep your focus on the benefit of all, magic happens.

There are all kinds of problems that can never be solved from the current points of view. Even at the greatest heights of conventional intellectual achievement, that's not what is going to solve the problem. However, for people who are committed to enlightened open intelligence as already accomplished, there is no problem, right? There's not a problem and there's not-not a problem. So, we deal with that.

We're not just practicing for a tiny little self; we're practicing for loved ones and for the benefit of all as well. Due to the sublime energy of wisdom and compassion, we can engage anyone fully where they are. The sublime energy of wisdom and compassion engages everyone where they're at, meeting them completely and dedicating our energy to whatever it is that's important to them. No one needs to be made different. Then, wherever we go throughout the day and whomever it is we meet, we know how to respond.

The generosity of friendship is to see all beings through pure perception, to perceive all beings—beings we can see and beings we can't see—through the eyes of pure perception and being committed to their enlightenment through any means whatsoever. We can know that those means are accessible and available and that it is not something that is in the distant future. Because we're all realizing it here together, it's the energy of what is actually taking place right here. It's that kind of energy that comes about through pure perception.

There is incredible confusion about enlightenment. To be perfectly clear, enlightenment is the end of suffering. That's what enlightenment is—the end of suffering. What happens then is a proliferation of generosity of all kinds. For example, teaching is a form of generosity. Showing up and sitting in the chair to listen to teachings is a form of generosity. Generosity—no stopping of generosity 24/7, and 24/7 the ending of suffering.

To be generous in this life means to take everything we know and commit it to the enlightenment of all. Now, it may not be that we're specifically teaching in a formal setting, but we're all teaching in some way, and we're all devoted to contributing in some way. Whatever our service may be, we are contributing. We're contributing from the devotion to an enlightened collective, not as some kind of harebrained idea, but as actuality.

A thought such as "wanting for others more than we wish even for ourselves" is an extraordinary and precious state of mind, and its occurrence a marvel unlike any other. It is generosity at its ultimate, a spontaneous largess of body, speech and mind. This is mind, speech and body in which any thoughts that occur are in service of everyone. This is an ultimate kind of generosity—in which we're included—because each of us is included in "everyone." Wishing for the enlightenment of all and aspiring to that opens up a flow of the indestructible heart essence.

Rest naturally; rest is best. We can rest naturally, and then we come to know what the qualities and activities of strong mind really are. There isn't any longer the exclusive interest in the self: "I'm this, I'm that, I'm the other thing, and I need to stand out from others." Instead, our whole life is about generosity—giving, giving, giving. It's a great joy to be grateful. Being grateful is an offering; it's an act of generosity.

There is the concept of a "gift economy," where resources and services flow from the vantage of generosity and generous giving, rather than merely as a tit-for-tat transaction. For me, the gift economy is an obvious form of enlightened energy. The more we practice, the more the gift economy comes about, but we have to be able to recognize what "a gift" is. Actually, our most precious gift is each moment of open intelligence. The great gift of enlightened energy is that it brings generosity to all beings; it brings harmony to all beings. Giving, giving, giving, giving— everything is done with the attitude of generosity, rather than merely getting something for oneself.

These gifts of enlightened energy's indestructible pride and indestructible dignity that pour forth are like sunlight from the sun. Those two terms—indestructible pride and indestructible dignity—are the same thing for our purposes. Indestructible dignity—what a gift! No matter what anyone says or does to you, you know exactly where you stand. You don't have to be concerned about what you need to say or do or anything else, because you know that it will come directly from open intelligence.

Without complete knowledge about what makes us tick, we can't possibly know how anyone else ticks. This is the gift as well: in order to be able to gift others with our wisdom and skillful means, first it needs to be applied to ourselves.

The greatest gift is considered to be sharing dharma—realization of open intelligence and sharing the dharma. We share the Teaching because it has a direct impact on all of life. We actually share the Teaching every time that we come from the vantage of open intelligence.

There are so many tremendous gifts that come about through practice. For instance, you can be in the middle of a situation that is going thousands of different crazy ways, and you just know exactly how to respond. Being ethical and moral doesn't mean being sweet and nice-y nice all the time.

It means that whatever you have to give, you will give honestly from the standpoint of wisdom and skillful means, but without having any preconceived idea of what that looks like. The only thing it looks like is whatever is most needed in that moment.

TONGLEN: THE COMPASSION OF TAKING AND GIVING

CHAPTER THIRTEEN

Giving—generosity—is so very important. There is a wonderful practice of generosity, and in Tibetan it is called "Tonglen." It is taking in all the suffering of others and giving out benefit and bliss. So, for example, say we are ill, and when we're ill we may feel like we are the only person in the world who is ill, and there is all of that self-focus because of the illness. But if we genuinely consider the number of people who are ill at the same time, and we take in their suffering and give out kindness, benefit and compassion, it really opens the heart of compassion so very deeply.

In accepting suffering from everyone, everywhere and giving away every sweet, wonderful and powerful thing about ourselves to everyone everywhere who has been suffering, that opens a tremendous space. That space cannot be accessed any other way than through heartfelt taking and giving. Through the Tonglen practice we will come to see that there is nothing else other than loving open intelligence.

Tonglen is so powerful; it goes totally beyond any kind of conceptual system. Because Bodhicitta cannot be realized conceptually, Tonglen is a wordless practice that allows this to occur. Bodhicitta is the living of life with only one point in mind, and that point is the enlightenment of all beings right now. That is the fruition of Bodhicitta, where all of one's qualities and activities come spontaneously from Bodhicitta without any effort. Going through one's day, Bodhicitta is always present.

Thinking about the past, present or future, it's always in relation to Bodhicitta.

To take in the world's suffering can be described in the following way: when you feel something like anger, doubt, hope, fear, jealousy, envy, arrogance, pride or whatever it might be, rather than feeling tight, constrained and violated by that thought or emotion, realize in that moment how many there are who are *feeling exactly the same thing at exactly the same moment.* If there is anger for you, how many are there who are feeling exactly the same anger in that instant? There are probably millions of people at that very moment.

This is what it means to take in all the world's suffering. In that moment of realization of the suffering of many, expansion occurs beyond an individuated self. "Oh, there are many people who are sick right now, not just me." The realization of this is so freeing.

Let's say that we test positive for the coronavirus. We would be rightfully upset about something like that, and it is the kind of extreme circumstance that could cause a lot of self-obsessive concern. So, in Tonglen practice, we think about everyone else who has the coronavirus. In doing so, we now have a community of the many people who are suffering from the virus. There is a connection with all the suffering caused by this virus that is sweeping the world. In doing so, amidst the crisis of a world health epidemic, there is a community.

We can think about all of our good qualities we've achieved, all our enlightened qualities and activities, and we give them all away. We give everything away to all the other people with the virus. The more we give away, the more we realize we just are as we are. It does not matter what we think about ourselves, and doesn't matter what we think about others; all is resolved. It's called "outshining;" everything is outshone by reality *as it is*.

The greatest benefit any of us can be during this time is to rest as strong mind. That is the greatest benefit for us personally and for everyone who is suffering in the pandemic. And the entire world is suffering now. Whether people are already sick or not, the whole world has gone into a spin of acknowledged suffering— fear, terror, horror, powerlessness, helplessness—feelings that can overwhelm beings.

Due to your precious commitment to open intelligence, you can practice Tonglen. You can practice it in a small way, a medium-sized way or a big out-of-the-box way. Tonglen is so beneficial to you individually and to all beings. Of all the prayers, sutras, tantras and practices I have had laid at my feet all of my life, to me Tonglen is the most exquisite of all practices.

To begin Tonglen in a small way is just fine if it feels too big to you to take in too much suffering and give out all your goodness to the people who are suffering. Giving, giving, giving—that's the end of suffering.

Usually it is suggested that one start out in a simple way. Say you have a cold and you're suffering. "Oh, when will I get over this cold? I've had it a week and I'm too sick to eat," on and on and on. The practice of Tonglen is to imagine others—or maybe even everyone else in the world—who also has a cold at exactly the same time, and that immediately opens everything up. From

Tonglen practice flows a connection with other beings, which is very, very beautiful. It's easier and easier to see that all of us are what could be called a communal symbiosis, rather than a bunch of separate people and nations trying to compete with one another. So, the surfing of the tsunami that we seem to be doing on our own is actually a group effort!

Tonglen is a very refined and beautiful practice, and the first time I did the practice, I had the flu, and I just thought, "I'm going to try Tonglen practice with the flu and see how that works." So, I felt all my symptoms of the flu, then I thought about everyone in the world who had the flu at the same time. Suddenly it wasn't just me with the flu; there was a community of flu-ers everywhere—a big bouquet of flu-ers! That opened my heart so much to feel the mutuality of suffering.

Tonglen provides such a tremendous opening. It can be a little scary at first to feel like we're giving away everything we have, when we've spent so much time getting what we have. Well, it's worth it! By giving away everything we take ourselves to be, we find something we didn't contrive and something we didn't hope to get, because it's so far beyond anything we could think about or hope for. Tonglen is a very, very useful practice, particularly because in the course of our lives we have gone through a reification boot camp, in which it was drilled into us that we are a separate "other" that must protect and preserve itself at all costs.

Tonglen practice, taking and giving, is so beautiful, so generous. The evidence and the obviousness of that in daily life is a true joy. We go beyond needing or wanting anything or anyone for ourselves, and in that we have the greatest freedom in life. It's not being cavalier and saying, "Oh, I don't need anything or anyone." It means *to not make any demands on life any longer*. We are who we truly are, and whatever happens is how it is and who we are.

The purpose of Tonglen practice is to open up an entirely different view of reality, of all that is. It shifts our perspective into alignment with the perspective—and where we *only* see everything through that perspective—that everyone is already enlightened. There is no one who is not enlightened.

"Confusion," now there you go, that's a good one, isn't it! How many people have felt confusion? Okay, so we're not alone in confusion. Who wouldn't be confused having had no idea of who they are from the beginning of life? Most of us grow up thinking we're a mistake somehow. When feeling confused, the Tonglen practice is to imagine everyone in the world who also feels confusion—equal to our confusion or even greater. We imagine all the people and all the conditions they're in that might be a source of extreme confusion, circumstances that are unlike anything we may have known.

There's so much suffering and so much confusion in the world, so we take all that confusion and bring it in. We take it into ourselves, every single bit of it, and then give out everything we have realized. We give out all the healing powers, enlightening powers, or whatever powers we believe we've achieved. We give it all away.

The Tonglen practice of taking in all the suffering of all beings and giving out to all beings isn't the usual transactional relationship in mercantile, tit-for-tat Western culture! A possible effect of Tonglen could be to radically alter the way one views the world—and not just in an intellectual way. Now, even just an intellectual insight can completely soothe a person; however, the actual realization is far beyond that. It completely changes one's view, and it also brings many extraordinary and ordinary qualities into play. This is the access to the mind of great bliss seeing emptiness.

So, if things like enlightened qualities and activities are spoken about, these come into play when all of what one thinks one is—everything one has taken oneself to be, everything one has gained, all fame, all fortune—is given away to the suffering. Tonglen is a very powerful practice, and it does bring total relief, but it does also take some daring!

Tonglen is the most exquisite of all practices. When we can exchange ourselves for others, we really start to feel that there is only one beating heart. There is in fact only one single beating heart, and all of us collectively are that beating heart.

DZOGCHEN: THE GREAT PERFECTION

CHAPTER FOURTEEN

Dzogchen means "Great Completion" or "Great Perfection" because it sees individuals as perfect; it always upholds the perfection of beings. In many cultures the assumptions are based on the idea that people are bad and that they need moral and ethical injunctions so that they will be good—when in fact they are innately complete and perfect. The purpose of the practice of Dzogchen is to show us that we are innately complete. Dzogchen is a Teaching that tells us that, and not only does it tell us that like many enlightenment Teachings do, Dzogchen has an exact method that delivers the result.

What "utter completion" means is the utter completion of intelligence. It also means great completion. It doesn't say "great ending"; it says "great completion." Even if we reflect on that only a little bit, we know that completion doesn't indicate end.

Dzogchen differs from other enlightenment Teachings in which there is no exact method that achieves a result. Dzogchen is the only Teaching that delivers the result through a specific known method that has been tested and preserved over thousands of years.

In short moments, repeated many times, open intelligence becomes obvious at all times. Short moments, many times, is the meditation of Dzogchen.

Dzogchen has many tools, with the primary tool being short moments. That practice helps us train our minds so that we don't put so much energy into thought and emotion. Through that practice we know for sure what's good for us. That's the way we live our lives, and that's the way we practice. We are less self-protective, less emotionally reactive, and we go from happiness to happiness, instead of from one desire for experience to another desire for experience. We let all of that be *as it is* and we go to happiness.

Dzogchen is the most comprehensive order of intelligence; however, it's something that most of us do not know about, because we have been taught to reify everything that occurs. One way of reifying is to operate from extremes. In other words, it could be a vantage of, "This is an abuse," or "It's not an abuse," or, "This is honorable," or, "It's not honorable." In Dzogchen there are no extremes. I could say things about, for instance, a certain politician or a notable event, but no matter how long I went on, I would never say, "Yes or no," because the most comprehensive order of intelligence is not based on extremes. It's not based on yes or no.

This Teaching that we are involved with is a Dzogchen Teaching with a name attached to it; others have other names.

In certain contexts, Dzogchen is still taught within Tibetan Buddhism, but in this Teaching it is taught independently of Tibetan Buddhism. In order to give everyone a sense of context and community, we talk about Dzogchen—because we are part of the Dzogchen community—but this is a unique expression, you could say, one that is understandable to a modern audience.

We have a very simplified approach to Dzogchen, and this simplified approach is something that was encouraged in me when I met my Guru, Wangdor Rimpoche. Traditionally this is called education in the nature of mind. Wangdor Rimpoche calls mind "loving open intelligence," and that is the term we use for the nature of mind.

We practice strong mind, which is called "Dzogchen" by some. Even though "strong mind" is a phrase I personally like very much and am totally infatuated with, it doesn't mean everyone in the world needs to use that term. Dzogchen is one flavor of what can be realized. It's all the same taste, but it has a lot of different flavors.

Great completion isn't something that's going to be reached in the future; everything is right now. There is no future. In Dzogchen we live as a whole, not as something divided.

My experience is one of short moments of meditation, and this is something that I began early in my life, because as a devotional Catholic I was steeped in prayer and meditation. I loved all the rituals, all the colors and the music, and I found it very beautiful. When I was about seven, I already knew that God is love. God is love—that's all there is. This too is what Dzogchen is. It's not a blanked-out state of awareness. It's awareness with a strong foundation in kindness and love. I think this is very important to cultivate in all ways possible.

By practicing short moments, more and more we see we are open intelligence pervaded by love. The love we feel is ours. Maybe right now we only sense a bit of the sublime quality we have and the knowledge of what we really are. We may see only a little, yet there is *so much more to come*!

The enlightenment Teachings have been given for tens of thousands of years. It isn't anything new, it just looked different in each culture where there was a Teaching. In each of these practices, there is a mystical Teaching of enlightenment, if someone can find it. No matter what it is—Hinduism, Judaism, Christianity, Buddhism, Islam—they all have mystical Teachings that state exactly this Dzogchen truth. However, it's not usually openly given like this, so I feel greatly fortunate. Thank you, Wangdor Rimpoche!

MIND OF GREAT BLISS SEEING EMPTINESS

This all-penetrating, unimpeded vast expanse of great bliss seeing emptiness is the key point of inexpressible and naturally inherent mind, beyond all extremes such as rising and ceasing, existing and non-existing. It is so beyond words and out of reach of mental inquiry; it is fresh, pure, sudden and beyond description.

For me the mind of great bliss seeing emptiness is the same as it is for everyone. The mind of great bliss seeing emptiness is not unique to individuals; it simply is *as it is*. Everyone is the mind of great bliss seeing emptiness, and no one is left out. With a lifestyle of resting as the mind of great bliss seeing emptiness, it doesn't mean thoughts or data streams have stopped; it just means that they are *not given priority*. Reification is not given priority, and more and more data are seen simply as the dynamic energy of the mind of great bliss seeing emptiness. The mind of great bliss is easy for everyone. You may have experienced bliss at some point, even if it's only for a minute or two, and so, you have a sense of what it is and can practice to make it more obvious.

"Wisdom" is a word that's mentioned quite a bit in contemporary society, but wisdom is often not really understood. In the Teachings on Dzogchen, wisdom is very specific, and it's called sublime wisdom, which is the wisdom associated with the mind of great bliss seeing emptiness. There can be no wisdom without the mind of great bliss seeing emptiness; all wisdom comes from the mind of great bliss seeing emptiness.

I'm so happy to report that due to my repeating *mind of great bliss seeing emptiness* at least a hundred times, you're guaranteed to never forget it! Repetition furthers open intelligence.

THE WISH-FULFILLING GEM

What is it that we want our human life to be? Do we want to go for ordinary human activity alone and wrap ourselves up in that, or do we want to come to know the wish-fulfilling gem of open intelligence?

We can be representatives of enlightenment and show the world what enlightenment is, whether people call it "enlightenment" or not. Even if people don't know much about enlightenment, they can see in our qualities and activities whether or not we are committed to beneficial activity.

The wish-fulfilling gem is to have open intelligence pointed out. We're born as loving open intelligence, but we have forgotten about it, so when it is introduced initially, it's a relief, because now we remember it! If it isn't pointed out clearly, then it's difficult to grasp, but when it is pointed out clearly by a Lineage Successor, that is what is called "transmission." My definition of transmission is "to evoke" or "evocation." "Transmit" sounds like there's more than one individual, so it really doesn't make sense as a translation, when it really is the *evocation of something already present.*

Through the practice of Dzogchen it is seen that one's subjectification of oneself and objectification of others is simply reification. So, not subject/not object and not-not subject/not-not object—"not and not-not"—in other words, beyond conception, beyond imagination and cannot be put into words. This is the wisdom exaltation and enlightened energy of Dzogchen.

The two areas of deep understanding—as-it-is-ness and spontaneous presence—if these aren't yet present for you, then that's an area where practice needs to be applied. The spontaneous presence of open intelligence becomes clear, where it's not only a realization but an ongoing experience twenty-four hours a day. So that, when you go to sleep at night, you go to sleep in open intelligence enlightened energy, and you wake up with that as well. Your last thought before going to sleep and your first thought in the morning are spontaneously this reality. This was most likely not demonstrated to us in our early life, because we only learned a conceptual reality. However, if we are lucky, we have received instruction, and now we have some greater sense of what reality might actually be.

In Dzogchen there is what is called a "thorough cut," which means a thorough cut through all conceptual boundaries, all reification. When that thorough cut is complete, then there is what is called "direct crossing." The thinking that has kept us in the grasp of reification can't get us out of that grasp, but the direct transmission of pure benefit cuts right through that and crosses over completely to a new intelligence. It cuts the root of reification and simultaneously crosses over—a direct crossing.

The Teachings do not bring any harm, none at all. I think everyone who is involved in Dzogchen would agree with that: the Teachings do not bring harm. When you're in a relationship with a teacher, a real relationship where both know the relationship is occurring, then there is a direct connection with what is real, and in this treasured relationship virtue, love, wisdom and benefit flourish and increase. There are pith instructions and practical methods that are implemented in conversations and interactions and in everything that occurs in the relationship.

THE PRACTICE OF DZOGCHEN

Training in Dzogchen is simply short moments of recognition of open intelligence, repeated many times, which is supported by Bodhicitta. Meditating on impermanence is something that people need to do before they turn their minds to Dzogchen, because it inspires and moves them to seek Dzogchen. Meditating on impermanence while practicing Dzogchen unfolds and increases the ability to be diligent, and finally it enables one to realize Dzogchen fully.

Dzogchen Teachings guarantee that even if there is no enlightenment for a practitioner, there is enduring happiness for the remainder of our lives. What a pleasure! Now, *that* I would call true pleasure! Add to that the assurance and confidence that comes from knowing that, no matter what storms may blow or waves there may be that look like they could drown us, this practice will carry us through.

In order for butter to be produced, the cream needs to be churned. This example is similar to how it is with the practice of short moments, many times. The more the cream is churned, the greater the likelihood that butter will be the result. Same-same: the greater the quantity of short moments, the greater the recognition of open intelligence.

But if we complicate things with lots of thinking, well, that is just because we have been trained to be conceptual thinkers. However, Dzogchen isn't about conceptual thinking; it's about open intelligence pervaded by love. Another word for that is compassion, but in Dzogchen it's called Bodhicitta, ultimate Bodhicitta. The love realized in Dzogchen is the love for everyone, and the mind in its own essence provides the greatest love and happiness that can ever be known. It also gives us the indestructible dignity and energy to spread that love everywhere.

I wanted to make perfectly clear that the Teaching does not mean to say that all data streams and all thoughts will disappear. The way it's stated in the Teaching is nuanced, which means that the thoughts and emotions *are seen as they are*. Data are easefully and spontaneously self-releasing for some people—and even for them maybe sometimes having a hold—and for others data have quite a firm hold. However, it doesn't change the *nature* of data as loving open intelligence. Data are the dynamic energy of open intelligence and inseparable from open intelligence. "Reification" means that reified data streams are seen as foremost; however, data always and forever remain inseparable and non-different from open intelligence.

The Teachings should not be given to people who have not been first prepared and then taken into profundity. That is definitely what occurs in the course of the practice—prepared and then taken into profundity. It may be that a person isn't prepared in Dzogchen, and they've had no specific training in that way. However, a person may have developed Bodhicitta elsewhere, and they may have had a life of complete service, one where they are devoted to something other than data streams. Then, when such a person is introduced to Dzogchen, the introduction is easier, because they have been living a life of Bodhicitta for many years—without even knowing to name it in that way. In those cases, the people are completely committed to whatever that Bodhicitta lifestyle is, rather than being committed to data streams.

Deep understanding of Dzogchen comes first. Second, the actual ability to leave everything *as it is*. The practice is to leave any negative state that arises *as it is* without going into a big story about it. There's a big distinction between the concept *as it is* and actually living *as it is*. Third is pure perception. These are holy words; this is a sacred phrase, among the holiest of the holy: pure perception. Everything is pure. Realization-or-no-realization, up or down, all around—everything is pure. The concept is surely gorgeous in itself, and yet the *practice* of pure perception is something entirely distinct. So, short moments of pure perception, repeated many times, and then too the pure perception becomes automatic.

Completely unexpected events are all part of impermanence, and we have to be able to think about everything without fear. So, say that all of a sudden because of a worldwide upheaval none of the usual offerings of the Teachings are available: no in-person meetings, no trainings and maybe we can't even come together with others in any way. But we can at least remember the Four Mainstays and hold to the practice of short moments. We can remember that there are texts online and ways to connect with people in a way that does not involve physical proximity.

Even with the many unexpected events of this present time, where so many of the usual practices are disrupted, it may be possible for some people to find the time and opportunity to devote themselves to the Teaching in a very profound way. So, those who are able to seclude themselves in retreat, even if it is only a short moment of retreat, they can put aside the worldly cares and activities of this life and practice single-mindedly, as directed by their teacher. Whatever the circumstance may be, gain liberation—in this very lifetime—in the ground of primordial purity. So, attain enlightenment in this very life!

When we introduced the concept of resting *as* awareness in the early 2000s, we changed the word "in," as in "resting *in* awareness," to "resting *as* awareness." That was a significant change, because with resting *in* awareness it seemed like there was a person resting and an object to be rested in. That simple change of preposition from "in" to "as" completely changed the meaning of the phrase. "Resting *as* awareness" means that the rester and the awareness are co-equal. They are equal and even and not separated because of there being a subject *in* awareness.

We also introduced "rest is best" and "resting naturally." Now all of these methods are used in practices all over the world, and not just in Buddhist or Dzogchen practices. It's something new that never occurred to most people before, and now it does. This also demonstrates how technologies and skillful means that are available now can be used to further the realization of open intelligence pervaded by love.

My Root Gurus have emphasized for us what is called "furtherance of Dzogchen." We don't even really need to call it Dzogchen, but we are Dzogchen practitioners, so we use that name. Furtherance of Dzogchen means betterment of Dzogchen, and "betterment of Dzogchen" isn't entirely focused on only one culture, and it is made accessible to more people all around the world.

Historically speaking, the vigilance related to furtherance of Dzogchen emerges from the authentic devotion, practice and realization of practitioners. Such displays are the spontaneous outflow and the natural flowering of a life lived in the primordial nature of open intelligence and love. It is from such sources that the truly fresh and vigorous creativity of Dzogchen has continued to unfold in the world.

With any new language or culture that is dissimilar to the culture we grew up in, at first it takes a while to become acquainted with that new culture and to grok its logic. And so it is with these Teachings, which were being sustained and cherished for thousands of years in a culture very different to our own.

These are very old Teachings, and all of the Dzogchen practitioners who have practiced Dzogchen for at least eighteen thousand years have practiced it in the same way. It's a very long Lineage, and all of these beings are present. They're right here in this room with us, and everywhere else too.

In Tibet there were very involved ways of making certain that this Dzogchen instruction would take place, and those ways largely do not apply to a global situation. This is what Wangdor Rimpoche meant when he invited us to "further Dzogchen" and to "better Dzogchen," because he knew that this would be the way that it would need to be in the future. He had lived in the circumstance in which the Teachings were developed and utilized in Tibet, and when he left Tibet he could see from his experience in India that Teachings were needed other than Teachings in a Tibetan system or setting. The Dzogchen Teachings are still necessary; however, they are in another format, because the Tibetan format may be pleasing only to a small number of people.

Devotion and practice are needed in order for enlightened energy to come about. Without devotion, there is no enlightened energy. Only by examining thoroughly all of the qualities and activities of enlightened beings is it possible for us to recognize the same enlightenment in ourselves.

The pith instructions of the Teaching encompass all of the Twelve Empowerments and all of the other Teachings. The pith instructions are absolutely essential. They are not based merely on words; they're based on our own practice and where our own practice really is. This is the Lineage Teaching; this isn't something I created. Everything I'm stating here is Lineage Teachings which are grounded in what works.

THE LINEAGE OF DZOGCHEN
CHAPTER FIFTEEN

The Lineage of Dzogchen isn't a line. It doesn't say "line-age"; it's a Lineage of the mind of great bliss seeing emptiness. In recognizing the mind of great bliss, we are lifted out of the confusion of taking ourselves to be a clot of reification, and we are opened into brilliance. This is the kindest we can be to ourselves.

When we look at all of human culture, what has been hidden from view and known only by a few now is open to view by many. The technology is available for so very many people all over the world to have it open to view.

Whenever there are new communication technologies, Dzogchen adapts to that in order to be more readily available. For example, when Padmasambhava came to Tibet with the Dzogchen Teachings, he looked carefully at what the situation was there, and he adapted to what was wanted and needed by the people. They had been practicing a shamanistic form of religion, so he put together Buddhism with the shamanistic form of religion. That's how Dzogchen became so colorful and unique. There was a period in Tibet where the Teachings weren't highlighted that much in the culture, but then they were reinvigorated due to the appearance of new technologies. There's nothing really "new" going on in Dzogchen now; it is just history repeating itself.

When there was only an oral history of transmission in Tibet and few books were available, the early masters carried small paintings with them so that they could show the metaphors, similes and analogies—the same metaphors that we still use in the present day! So, when they referred to "a rainbow in the sky" or "the sky and the color blue," they would hold up the painting of that image. Nowadays we have many ways of presenting the symbols of Dzogchen, and we've done this extensively online already. There are many possible methods of presentation of Dzogchen.

Through the practice of Dzogchen, what would have been our thought or our disposition about a situation through reification is now informed by open intelligence; it is spontaneously informed by what is best, and not only for us as individuals, but for everyone collectively. That's what we can do—practice open intelligence, strong mind.

In the Four Mainstays, we focus on the well-being of the group. We naturally gravitate towards each other; we find great comfort in Dzogchen family, in all Dzogchen family. We notice this with Tibetan practitioners, and we want to learn from them, "How can we be Dzogchen practitioners, too?" Even for us Westerners—with our bent towards logic, reason, the scientific method and in our being so prideful about our culture as if it were the only one—we want to learn more.

DZOGCHEN GOES OUT INTO THE WORLD

When the great Dzogchen Lamas fled from Tibet, they had no idea what was going to happen, not in that moment or over the course of time. They had no idea that Dzogchen would be spreading all over the world. That was unknown to most of them, unless they had had specific visions about what the future would bring. This change of geographical circumstance is very important to understand, because the Dzogchen community went from being an unknown community within a very small part of human culture to one that is affecting human culture worldwide.

We are so blessed to have Tibetan teachers throughout the world now—Tibetan masters, Dzogchen masters. Most of us would have never heard of anything like this if there had not been the Cultural Revolution and the expulsion of the Tibetans from Tibet. By killing a million inhabitants the Chinese took so much from Tibet, but it resulted in sending people all over the world to teach Dzogchen. That's Dzogchen energy. Like for example Wangdor Rimpoche step-by-step carrying his Guru on his back from Tibet to India—that is enlightened energy one step at a time.

This is a time of great change for the Teachings. Many great teachers now are saying that Tibetan Buddhism will possibly come to an end. How could they go through all this—being persecuted, imprisoned and having to flee their country because of invasion by another country—and then say so candidly that Tibetan Buddhism may disappear? Is this a forecast of doom? No, it isn't a forecast of doom. With the Teachings of Dzogchen now spreading all over the world, it is a forecast of the very, very best for not only all of human society, but any beings that exist.

This is leading to the enlightenment of the collective. There will be a point at which enlightenment no longer needs to be elected or aspired for; it will come about spontaneously throughout the culture.

A cooperative community of Dzogchen practitioners who are speaking English, Tibetan and many other languages brought Dzogchen reality to the world at large. This is a definitive community throughout the world of all kinds of people. Even with the destruction of so many monasteries in Tibet, there was no way that the Dzogchen community could be extinguished. Despite the actions of hostile political forces, Dzogchen wasn't extinguished. Instead, what happened? It spread all over the world.

As a result of the Chinese occupation of Tibet, there were Dzogchen Lamas who were marched off to prison and who stayed there for twenty years or even longer. There were masters of Dzogchen who went to prison, but also many other people. These were practitioners and other kinds of people who had realized buddha-qualities—doctors, lawyers, traders, wandering mendicants, all kinds of people—and they too were put into prison. All of these people who survived the ordeal did so only due to Dzogchen practice, and if they died, they died in the reality of Dzogchen, great completion, the great union of appearances and emptiness.

Many of my friends had to flee Tibet with great hardship. The difficult journey from one country to the other took months, and they have said that they were able to do it due to their faith in open intelligence. The ordeal increased their faith in open intelligence because they needed to stay with open intelligence all the while, no matter what happened. They saw others who did not have that faith during the journey who would commit suicide or who would turn back. With the fear of going forward or the fear of no longer being able to live the way they always had, many would turn back, knowing full well that it meant their death or imprisonment. For those who persevered, faith in open intelligence saved their lives and the lives of many others. It's in that context that we talk about faith and belief. It's a faith and belief that aren't demanded; it's an invitation or opportunity that is introduced.

A great way to look at fear when fear comes up is that, even in fear, there is fearlessness. There are many people who have experienced incredible fear, who had to flee their native land in very harsh conditions and with soldiers shooting at them. These are people I actually know, people who lived with incredible fear beyond what most of us would ever experience, and in this fear there was complete fearlessness. There was increasing gratitude for the fearlessness that is always present. It was not just fearlessness in the face of one's enemies, but all-around general fearlessness, a fearlessness related to spontaneous wisdom benefit and the spontaneous willingness of mind, speech, body, qualities and activities to do what needs to be done for the benefit of all.

An Unbroken Lineage

We rely on what the most experienced persons have relied on. We have the whole Lineage of teachers and all of their Teachings as well. We rely on the same Teaching that brought them to enlightenment and brought millions of other people to enlightenment. From that we gain strength. This enlightenment was and is possible for the entire Lineage, and we are part of that Lineage. You could say that the Lineage is with us at all times. This is an unbroken Lineage.

This is a Lineage that has stayed specifically with its key points and pith instructions down through the ages, one which has written all of the key instructions down or passed along an oral history. Biographies and autobiographies have been created so that every person who reads them can see what they're capable of through the examples of the great Dzogchen masters. Dzogchen is the only philosophical tradition in the world that has descriptions of the lives of each of their masters—where they were born, special signs at their birth, the Teachings they received during their life, the Dzogchen master who gave them those Teachings, then the extraordinary, sublime siddhis (*extraordinary powers*) that they were able to demonstrate due to their realization.

Great wisdom exaltation and sublime enlightened energy are informed by Guru-Lineage, Bodhicitta Mind and spontaneous great bliss seeing emptiness. Each one of these terms is very specific and filled with sublime power—what in Sanskrit is called a "siddhi." But this isn't just an ordinary siddhi, this is an extraordinary siddhi. It means a "sublime power," because the entire notion of what mind, body, and speech are is taken over completely by spontaneous great bliss seeing emptiness.

The Guru-Lineage in an ultimate sense, in the ultimate Bodhicitta sense, means to enlighten all beings, not just sometime in the future, but right now, and we hold ourselves to account for that. If enlightenment is in fact already present, then why not? Why not rely on the open intelligence that is here right now? Just as you can be enlightened, so everyone can be enlightened.

One Tibetan master was asked what the most difficult thing was that he faced after many years in a Chinese prison, and he said, "Retaining compassion for the Chinese." We can see with some of the feelings we might have today about different political figures and the challenging circumstances so many face around the world that we each have our particular view about those things. We can easily maintain a view throughout life about all kinds of reified things, but whatever that view might be for any one of us, how much easier it is to have a life filled with strong mind rather than suffering.

MILAREPA

Milarepa was one of the greatest Dzogchen masters in Tibet, but early on in his life he killed thirty-eight of his relatives out of revenge. He had tremendous remorse for this deed and he was inspired to change, and once he was inspired to change, he was fully inspired and fully motivated. He knew where to go after the murdering was complete. He had the full intention to practice Dzogchen and to receive instruction, but it was a long time before he ever actually received the Teachings. He had a Dzogchen Guru, but he had to prove himself first. Eventually he received teachings and became one of the greatest masters ever. Milarepa obeyed all of his Guru's instructions and considered them to be the true dharma.

Through his example we can see that even someone who had an entirely immoral past can be suddenly open. The openness is key, the openness to instinctively recognize awareness—open intelligence, strong mind—right here. Through that, perfect strength and perfect stability come about, and the need to get into specific data streams and think they're real completely dissolves. This taking-unreal-things-to-be-real just isn't there anymore, and all there is is sublime and all-resounding, compassionate, wisdom energy.

WANGDOR RIMPOCHE

When the circumstances in Tibet became even more threatening in 1959, it was clear to Wangdor Rimpoche that it was no longer safe to remain there, and his focus turned to finding a way to get his Guru, Thuksey Rinpoche, out of danger. Wangdor Rimpoche would not leave Tibet unless his Guru could come with him. Others struck out on the journey on their own, but Wangdor Rimpoche refused to leave Thuksey Rinpoche behind. He tried all kinds of means to transport his Guru. He hired some mountain men to try to carry Thuksey Rinpoche, but he was very large and the mountain men couldn't carry him. Then they yoked yaks together, but they couldn't carry him either.

Wangdor Rimpoche decided, "I'm not leaving unless he leaves, and I'm going, so I will carry Thuksey Rinpoche to India," and that is what he did; he carried him. One moment at a time, one short moment at a time, he carried his Guru all the way from Tibet to India on his back. Just the process of getting through all the Chinese posts was an incredible effort. Along the way they lost all of their pack animals, and out of the whole group that left, only seven people made it all the way to India.

Wangdor Rimpoche considers this his greatest accomplishment, as it preserved Dzogchen Teachings and Transmissions of enlightened energy only held by Thuksey Rinpoche. His Guru was the head of what is called the Drukpa Kagyu Lineage, and Wangdor Rimpoche said that if he had not carried his Guru, all of the Teachings that his Guru held in his heart would have been lost forever.

I was astounded when I heard this story. I thought, "I have so much reverence for him and faith in his ability," faith not just in his aspiration, but in his activities and qualities that are all for the benefit of beings. This is what Guru Yoga is.

In contemplating this story for many years, I know why Rimpoche said it was his greatest accomplishment. It is a testimony to short moments—that in short moments, one step at a time, we have everything it takes to open our entire concept of love beyond anything we ever conceived possible. Why would Wangdor Rimpoche risk his own life to carry his Guru who was twice his size on his back for a journey he knew would take months? Because he *is* his Guru, and his Guru gave him everything—everything needed to open his intelligence into one of pure love and pure intelligence.

After the journey, Wangdor Rimpoche was in hospital for one year in Mumbai, and then he wandered north to his new home in the holy caves of Padmasambhava. Here other lifelong Dzogchen practitioners, mostly Tibetan, gathered around him to live and practice in permanent retreat. Wangdor Rimpoche travelled the world for thirty years, his only purpose being the introduction of the Dzogchen view, meditation and action. Due to the devoted service of people like Wangdor Rimpoche, the Dzogchen Lineage is now taught globally, adapting to time and place, yet without reliance on time and place, providing the enlightened

energy for realization of the sublime meaning of human nature—
open intelligence and love.

MINLING TRICHEN RINPOCHE

Minling Trichen Rinpoche lived with his family in Tibet, and they didn't talk about Guru Yoga or the Mindrolling family Lineage, but he knew that his father was a Guru. When he was eight years old his father died, and he inherited this enormous Lineage that dates back thousands of years. As the Lineage Holder he needed to begin to memorize the Teachings, and within just a couple of months he had to memorize a thousand pages of Teachings, and then as an eight-year-old boy recite it to a group of people. This is how he began his life as a very important Guru.

Like many other Tibetans, he had to leave Tibet, and when they left they had nothing; they were absolutely poor. But none of that stood in the way; no thought like that could ever deter what he saw in front of him. He built a great monastery in Dehradun in India, and he was able to do all of this through his aspiration and action to benefit beings, to enlighten the collective. Another word for that is Bodhicitta. That is what Bodhicitta means—not just aspiration, but also *action* to benefit all beings and to enlighten the collective. He didn't think about anything else, and the same is true with Wangdor Rimpoche. Their way of being is aspiration and action to benefit all.

I met Minling Trichen Rinpoche just prior to meeting Wangdor Rimpoche, and each time I met with him, I met with him alone. He taught only in Tibetan, and by the time I met him he wasn't teaching large groups. When I met him, I didn't realize what an honor it was to meet with him alone, but very quickly I did. I could see just by looking at the monastery and the stupa, and I could feel in my heart, that he had the benefit of all and the enlightenment of the collective in mind, and that this was all he had in mind.

Nyoshul Khenpo Rinpoche

Nyoshul Khenpo Rinpoche was a very great Dzogchen master, one of the greatest Dzogchen masters who ever lived. In Tibet he had sat on a golden throne and taught thousands, including many other Rinpoches. Like so many others, he had to leave Tibet, and after the long journey from Tibet to India he was left with nothing. He became a sadhu (*renunciate monk*) in Rishikesh, and he was constantly depressed and sick. There was nowhere to go at the time for Tibetans living in exile, and he heard that there were jobs in Calcutta, so he went to Calcutta and became a dishwasher in a hotel. He continued to be depressed and sick. He was asked once, "So, if you were depressed and sick, how does that match up with the Teachings? How can you be a Dzogchen master and be depressed and sick?" He said, "Being depressed and sick? All it has done is to increase my faith in the Teachings."

The Teachings are an incredible resource. One knows that whatever is occurring is for the benefit of all, even though it may not seem obvious at the time—with no fear about the future and no hope about what it might bring. This is all-centered beneficial potency, where no matter the disruption in our life, faith never wavers. The obviousness of beneficial potency is so great that it is always on and it can never be knocked off base. How did he get to this point in his life? He got there through devotion to his Guru.

This great being, Nyoshul Khenpo Rinpoche, had stored in his mind the entire history of the Lineage and over a thousand biographies of different great beings who have attained open intelligence's all-centered beneficial potency. In his mind was every detail of their lives, what the special signs were at their birth that indicated they were a great being, every single Teaching they ever had, who they had the Teaching from, and what exactly were the signs that they demonstrated that confirmed them as a great being. All of this was stored in his mind.

His Guru was a great, great being, and the Guru knew that this collection of biographies was crucial to the whole systematic methodology of the Tibetan historical system. Nyoshul Khenpo Rinpoche itemized and recorded these incredible biographies in a way that would enrich the Teachings and bring them alive for every generation that came thereafter.

THE GURU,
DISPELLER OF DARKNESS
CHAPTER SIXTEEN

Guru devotion is considered to be not only the swiftest way, but also the easiest way to enlightenment. Earlier on in my life, I didn't think that Guru devotion could possibly happen for me. It was just not a part of any kind of conceptual framework that I held, and I didn't understand how seeing the Guru as a living-buddha could in any way inspire me in enlightenment or support anyone else in enlightenment. I was wrong. Even if before I didn't believe a word of this whole devotion thing, when I met my Guru Wangdor Rimpoche, I felt spontaneous devotion. I felt reality— "Real, this is real!"

I had met many masters before I met Wangdor Rimpoche, and I had had an opportunity to have conversations with them as well, but when I met Wangdor Rimpoche, *boom*, that was it! I felt spontaneous Guru devotion, and I understood everything he said. Not only did I understand it as an experience, but I actually realized it.

The Guru emphasizes our goodness; the Guru sees us as perfectly good. So, if the Guru believes that we don't recognize our own goodness, the Guru can be raw and say things that perhaps initially may seem harsh, or they give us a project to take on that just seems completely beyond our scope and capacity. However, whatever it is, it is because the Guru has complete confidence in our capacity. The Guru does not see us as being different from or other than what they are. What more beautiful form of loving support could there be than this when facing whatever tsunami may be coming at us. Surfing with accompaniment, one could say!

Some people become afraid even when they hear the word "Guru"! They think, "Oh, Gurus, I've heard all these bad things about what Gurus do. They might do this or that; they might take advantage of me sexually or they might push me off a mountain, or, or . . ." Maybe things like that have happened, I don't know. I only know about my own Guru. My own experience is that my Guru exalts me, and "to exalt" means there is the vivid presence of the end of suffering along with indestructible dignity. Not pride or arrogance, but indestructible dignity in knowing who we are and what our strengths, gifts and talents are and how we can share our strengths, gifts and talents with everyone.

The realization of sublime wisdom and indestructible dignity is so much greater than any kind of subjectively contrived experience. There has to be not just the introduction, but the introduction through the Lineage of Transmission for it to be a true introduction. The best of writings can be a tremendous support, but the words can never state what true realization is. Just as Wangdor Rimpoche says, transmission does not go into words.

The first phase—a proper introduction—carries with it some kind of reverence and faith in the Guru; that's just the way it is. The teacher automatically receives some kind of reverence and faith, even if at first it is only a token amount. Faith, trust and devotion, all of these are essential. Initial faith is developed through introduction. Faith is cultivated in your own experience. It isn't a conceptual faith; instead, it's a realization of faith itself—an upwelling of faith and gratitude. Initial faith in the Teaching itself is essential, and from that, usually with experience, devotion presents itself. As realization develops and reaches completion, more and more we see the benefit of the Guru. This is my own experience.

"Direct realization" means the realization of wisdom qualities and activities, so that all of one's energy is completely inseparable from the energy of the vast expanse and all love and compassion, all wisdom body, wisdom speech, wisdom mind, wisdom qualities and wisdom activities. These all pour forth from the compassionate energy of shining open intelligence. This is what wisdom is.

It is absolutely key to have a relationship with a Guru who has Lineage and who has the actual Teachings of the Lineage that have not changed for eons and which have brought realization to an exhaustless number of beings.

There's no separation between the student and the Guru. The Guru is present, and it is the Guru who is speaking, not an individual human being—Guru, Guru, dispeller of darkness. Guru Yoga is the one hundred percent always-on warmth and affection of open intelligence and love. So, instead of trying to focus on names or terms or descriptions, just practice Guru Yoga.

It is very important to understand that love and devotion to the Guru is not merely a person-to-person thing. It is not personal, like the love and devotion of one person for another. Everything is the Guru.

PRACTICES OF GURU DEVOTION

Short moments of Guru Yoga repeated many times . . . For those of you who have a Guru, please never be separate from Guru Yoga. I can't explain why it works or how, but I know it does.

When one hears the phrase "taking refuge," that means to take refuge in the mind of great bliss seeing emptiness, rather than having refuge in data reification. It's very simple. Taking refuge is a commitment. Usually to take refuge is a very formal process, possibly involving a ritual or ceremony, but it does not have to be that way. We take refuge in loving open intelligence, so this is the basis of the practice. We take refuge in the mind of great bliss seeing emptiness, and we use whatever our chosen tool is to do that.

Who is our primary target of propaganda and self-contempt? Ourselves. Who are we thinking about most of the time? Ourselves. So, we could say that we are very good at thinking about someone repetitively! It's true. We've been completely devoted to this self-focus practically since the day we were born. We definitely have a commitment to the self, and we've been convinced that we need to get that self pumped up and going at full speed to the degree that everyone else will notice us!

So, very simply, Guru Yoga, the thought of the Guru, just replaces that. But say that you just can't get into Guru devotion.

Well, how about one minute at a time of Guru devotion or an hour or a day? What could it cost you?

I want to share this with you because, as you can see, I'm very inspired by Guru Yoga and its gifts. I started out with faith, trust and reverence for the Guru, and that was a good foundation. Then I thought, "Well, I'm going to try devotion too." I simply started relating to my Guru's ordinary daily activities and seeing everything about my Guru as complete realization.

The importance of the Guru is their capacity to introduce open intelligence in a way that is simple, direct and all-inclusive—and terrifying! It's like an enormous eraser made of light, erasing everything into brightness. The tradition in Guru Yoga is to practice Guru Yoga at least once a day. What that can mean is, as soon as the eyes open in the morning, that's the signal to practice Guru Yoga. Or maybe you dream about the Guru, that's great too! So, as many times as possible during the day, remember the Guru. The first thing I do when I wake up is to think of the Rinpoches, and then this can move on to thinking of everyone—everyone I've ever known who is a practitioner, all sublime beings, all the Lineage Holders everywhere who have ever been—all present in that moment.

Most of you have relationships with people who have been close to you all of your lives. Maybe some of you have a strong family connection and you're really close to them, so you know what it means to have that kind of relationship. And so, these relationships with other people in life with whom you are close are really the basis for understanding the relationship with the Guru. These relationships with other people, how do they come about? You meet someone or have someone in your life and you deepen the relationship, and then you start to think about them, right? It's kind of hard to have a relationship if you never think about the person.

So, in regard to my own relationship with my Guru, I simply started to think about him and his daily life. That's what I did until the presence of the Guru became obvious at all times. Guru devotion is the result, which is to recognize the inseparability with the Guru, the indivisibility with the Guru and the Guru's realization. I began this path of devotion through these simple steps, and I'm sharing it with you to encourage you to really think about the Guru and about their life. What is their life like? What are they doing moment-to-moment? Yes, thinking about the Guru.

It is absolutely important to have motivation and intention. Everything you do in your life requires motivation and intention, so you already know what motivation and intention are. Applying motivation and intention to Guru Yoga is essential. It is a matter of the *quantity* of moments of devotion and not the quality. The perception of the Guru is constantly changing according to subjective judgments, so the quantity of moments of devotion is key. Whatever it requires—pictures of the Guru, having a screensaver of the Guru, having some other specific form of practice of Guru Yoga—quantity not quality. To me it's just a total pleasure to see the Guru everywhere, with each instant of Guru Yoga as the full flourishing of incomprehensible love and devotion.

The easiest Guru Yoga is to see every single action, activity and thought of the Guru as buddha. We have been trained that we are impure, when in fact we are pure, and the Guru always sees us as pure. There's no time the Guru does not see us as pure. When we see the Guru and all of their qualities and activities as pure—which is what it means to merge our mind with the Guru—we then come to see ourselves and all of our data as pure as well.

Most important is to cherish the precious moment of Guru-remembrance. If you take a bite of food, remember the Guru. If you are going to bed, remember the Guru. If you are getting up from bed, remember the Guru. If you do anything, remember the Guru. This is what I have found to be fruitful. It's a practice I never imagined myself doing, not ever. However, I am very willing to say, "I was completely wrong about my initial assumptions." I'm very happy and grateful that I could be open to this Teaching. To me it is the greatest blessing of my life. Whatever my presence is for, I want it to benefit you and make you happy.

The mind of great bliss seeing emptiness is raw, open and completely profound. The mind of great bliss comes about in Guru devotion. The mind of great bliss comes about because Guru devotion is inescapable. It makes it impossible to not love. That's what Guru devotion is: it makes it impossible to not love! That comes about in the moment, whatever it is. Initially, the instruction is to see the Guru as buddha. But what does that mean? Practically it means that in every thought of the Guru there is the realization that the Guru is evidence of buddha-qualities and activities.

One of the things I can state about Guru Yoga is that it is never finished, and the Guru isn't just left behind at some point. It doesn't matter what the realization is, because the realization is based on this intense, immense love that comes about through Guru Yoga. It is so extraordinary and so pervasive of everything in life, and it never goes away. The presence of the Guru is so obvious, no matter what the realization is. It can be the most extraordinary enlightenment that ever was, and the Guru will still be there pervasive of everything. This gives an idea of the all-pervasiveness of love and what enlightenment really is.

Wisdom and discernment are love, and love contains all kinds of wonderful aspects—not limited aspects, but pervasive. All aspects are all-pervasive. There is not just a little part of open intelligence over there somewhere; it is all-pervasive. This was one of the first teachings my teacher gave me. All-pervasiveness, Svābhāvikakāya.

My teacher Wangdor Rimpoche doesn't speak English, but I've learned to mostly understand what he says. He once was standing by a large window looking out to the ocean. He pointed outside and said "Svābhāvikakāya." The birds were flying by and leaving no trace and there was the sky with all its blueness, its openness, its spaciousness and its all-pervasiveness. There's no way to separate air and space, no way to separate sky and space, no way to separate any of these from loving open intelligence. Loving open intelligence, all-pervasive.

There can be data streams like, "Oh, these things in my mind are really bugging me. My consciousness, oh, if I could just get rid of that consciousness that's between mind and open intelligence, then I'd have it made." However, mind is a data stream, as is consciousness. There are no platforms called "these things." "These things" are data streams, made-up things. I've found that the way it works is to rely on the Guru—to have respect, faith, reverence, trust, devotion for the Guru, and to really be open to what that is and what that profoundly means. Guru Yoga is a profound passageway.

CLEAR-LIGHT-AWARENESS BODHICITTA

Guru Yoga is the skillful means for full Bodhicitta to be enriched. The word "Guru" means the dispeller of darkness and the bringer of light. A Guru is heavy with enlightened qualities and activities. Yoga means union, so through the Guru we are united in complete love. That love is not just any kind of love we've experienced already, like being in love with someone romantically or being in love with one's child. It is a love that is very directed, and that love is to see the Guru as buddha. Not buddha as a stone statue or a historical figure, but buddha-hood, the enlightenment that is latent in everyone, waiting to be fully expressed.

We proceed into the arena of the unthinkable and the unknowable. Mental activity becomes a seamless tool that might be drawn on a little bit here and there, but it is clear-light-awareness Bodhicitta that increasingly becomes our tool of vast illumination, our vast love for all being. All of this comes from the simplicity of Guru Yoga—moment-to-moment realizing that the Guru is buddha and the realization that seeing the Guru as buddha is the cure that erases ills, no matter what our illness might be—physical, mental, things we say, things we do.

It's in Guru Yoga that Bodhicitta is born. Bodhicitta means to see everything through pure perception. This is gradually born through Guru Yoga, through realizing that everything the Guru has to say is sublime wisdom. Everything that the Guru requests is sublime wisdom. Even if the Guru requests something of me that I see as completely impossible, still I show up. I realized that whatever the Guru requested of me will be born in wisdom, and I'll know what to do and how to act, even though it might seem like a stretch beyond anything I ever could have conceived.

ENTERING A RELATIONSHIP WITH A GURU

CHAPTER SEVENTEEN

When it comes to realization of what our wisdom qualities and activities are, a one-to-one relationship with the Guru is absolutely essential, because the Guru sets the mark so far beyond anything that we may think we're capable of, and we can no longer resort to merely ordinary ways of being. It's important to rely on the support of the Guru, because the energy is so immense and so new. This is very key.

Seeing the Guru as buddha can be very challenging. Often the Guru just does whatever it is they do, and it's totally up to us whether we realize the fruit in that or not. People are afraid sometimes of Guru devotion and make up all kinds of ideas and stories, and they look up things on the Internet and so forth. I had a graduate degree in that, too! I was an intellectual skeptic. I thought that things like Guru devotion were from feudalistic times or even further back; however, I was wrong. I'm happy to be wrong today, whereas at one time being wrong did not cause me happiness.

I would say that one of the distinctions between Guru devotion and other types of practice is that other types of practice can be dry. However, with Guru devotion, just thinking about the Guru is terrific and brings such joy, and it's not merely intellectual. It doesn't have any conceptual framework. It definitely alleviates all fear. So, that's great if this is your practice.

152

The only role of the Guru is to push, push, push, but that requires entering into a close relationship. It doesn't mean just writing to them or listening to what they say, although that's good too. It really means wanting to participate in the flow of enlightened energy and being willing to be pushed wherever you don't want to go.

There are powers that we know very little about, but human beings are extraordinarily capable—so much more capable than we've allowed ourselves to be. To have the mentor, to have the great master, to have the holy blessed Guru living in one's heart is just the best way to live.

From my perspective, the relationship with the Guru is absolutely necessary, just so absolutely necessary. The realization of wisdom exaltation and sublime enlightened energy comes from Guru Yoga and from union with the Guru.

NOTHING AS LOVING OR INCREDIBLE AS GURU DEVOTION

In contemporary times it may seem a leap for us to elect something like Guru devotion, yet the fruits of it are so wondrous and sublime. The power to practice comes from Guru Yoga. Remembering the Guru throughout the day brings to life their always-presence. Gradually it is realized that there is no division between the Guru and one's own realization. Again, usually this comes about gradually, gradually.

We are *not* confined in a specific body-mind. Our body, speech and mind are inexhaustible. Intellectually we may know that we are not confined to a skin suit, yet our actual experience of that spaciousness—one hundred percent and on a daily basis—may not be fully ripened. Guru Yoga is about fully ripening that into completion.

When body, speech and mind are not fully aware and grounded in strong mind, they are just running around helter-skelter. We have no idea how easeful the relationship to body, speech and mind can be, and we think that helter-skelter is the only way it can be. "Oh, we're just human beings, so we're completely at the whim of all that," and we feel that we really don't have the tools to resolve it. However, the easiest way to resolve it is through Guru Yoga.

Because most of us hear about open intelligence for the first time from a self-cherishing place—in terms of cherishing our separate sense of self—it's very important to have some notion of what we're getting into, and this is where Guru devotion comes in. We replace "self-cherishing" with "Guru devotion"—something inconceivable, something that no one will ever be able to put their finger on. Guru devotion may be evoked or pointed out, but that doesn't mean that it can be defined, because it never is definitive. It is always opening up more in pure knowledge.

What is born in the relationship with the Guru is the capacity to see the Guru as the manifestation of sublime wisdom and compassion, and then also the capacity to enliven enlightenment in oneself and in the collective. This is my experience, and in this I have been able to see everything about my Guru as evidence of buddha-hood, so that all of what the Guru is appears as a glistening mandala (*a geometric figure representing the universe in Buddhist symbology*). No matter what it is—a glistening mandala. And there's never really any way of determining how that's going to look. All qualities and activities of sublime wisdom are born in particular circumstances, and as we know, these shift from instant to instant.

Guru devotion really inspires the inseparability of immense love and compassion that is embodied in open intelligence. It's inspired through an actual experience in our own life with a living being, and the living being—the Guru—is an expression of the Lineage. To engage in Guru Yoga means to have open intelligence that is warmed up and increasingly obvious. When any of us are going through a bleak period, it's very important to practice—to write out the text, listen to a talk, to practice Guru devotion. There is nothing as soothing, as charming, as loving or as incredible as Guru devotion to support us in surfing whatever tsunami is coming our way. The trust and devotion are what will carry us through.

The master responds according to what is needed by the students, not by some cooked-up formula. Everything is for the students. Teacher=students, students=teacher, a single body of equalness and evenness.

We feel more like we're resting inseparably as the dynamic energy, the sublime energy of the Guru. That doesn't mean that we should at some point discard the Guru, "Oh, I've got it now, so I can throw the Guru away," because the Guru is the sublime energy of wise and compassionate action.

"A devotional longing" is an expression of wanting to be more and more ourselves, more and more who we really are.

When someone asks for a blessing, what the original word "blessing" means when used in Sanskrit is "energy." So, it is, "I pray for enlightened energy," or, "Holy Guru, please share your enlightened energy with me." It isn't a matter of a "high one" doing something for a "low one." It is just a matter of someone who has practiced more or longer sharing enlightened energy.

ZIJI RINPOCHE'S OWN PRACTICE OF GURU YOGA

Initially the Teaching is to see the Guru as buddha. But what does that mean? It means practically, that in every thought of the Guru there is the realization that the Guru is buddha. In my case it could be easier to do so because there were so many people who already recognized Wangdor Rimpoche as a living-buddha when I met him. I knew that if there was something in error in my perception that it was definitely on me and not on him. But I didn't have a lot of those thoughts of trying to make sense of things.

Every single thing that would make a person think that someone *isn't* a buddha, all of that has to come up, or there's no way to penetrate through it. That's one of the roles of the Guru; the Guru has to be present and completely naked, so to speak, the living example of everything being included in realization. This is why the Teachings state very clearly to include practice in all activities.

I had grown up in a very devotional household, so I knew what devotion was, or I thought I did. I would eventually read whatever I could find on devotion to the Guru, and what I found was that the easiest approach is just to think about the Guru—to think about the Guru and kind of reorganize my thinking.

There are ordinary beings, there are practitioners and there are sublime beings. Just to benefit myself on this journey, I'm going to say that this person to whom I am devoted, my Guru, is a sublime being. So, just with rational thinking and reason I could easily qualify the person as a sublime being—this person out of the ordinary, a sublime being. I had never known beings like these before. So, I felt very willing to enter through the doorway of clear-light devotion.

In terms of my own experience of reverence for the Guru and faith in the Guru, I can share something with you here. In the past I was not one to believe in Guru Yoga at all. To me, intellectually it just seemed like something that belonged in the past in some kind of a culture where people believed in superstition. That was exactly my definition, and so I did not in any way aspire to Guru Yoga or think that it would be part of my life, not ever.

I met many Gurus, and then I met Minling Trichen Rinpoche and Wangdor Rimpoche, and I had an incredible amount of respect for both of these beings from the very beginning. I had so much respect just out of hearing their stories of what their lives had been like. For instance, Wangdor Rimpoche carried his Guru on his back all the way from Tibet to India. He says that this is his greatest accomplishment and that if he had not carried his Guru, all of the Teachings that his Guru held in his heart would have been lost forever.

Wangdor Rimpoche carried his Guru from Tibet to India and through that taught me that anything is possible. It's only the limitation of my own reification that stands in the way. So, if I say something like, "To end suffering," then I have to ask myself, "What does ending suffering really mean?" Its profound meaning is the enlightenment of all *being*, not all beings—the enlightenment of all *being*. So, through his ways of teaching, here I sit.

Guru Yoga for me is twenty-four hours a day. There isn't any division anywhere. Guru Yoga is where it's at for me! Guru Yoga is not about being distant from someone else and appraising how they're doing or appraising how we're doing. It's a commitment. Little by little the relationship grows, and how we're doing in the relationship is something not only recognized by us, but also the teacher recognizes exactly how we're doing. This has been my experience.

The qualities and activities all come about through Transmission; this is my direct experience. I never feel particularly like I'm doing anything; I feel more like a recorder of timeless wisdom. In terms of the instructions, I am carrying the message of the Lineage, and the message is already set out and is perfectly clear.

Wangdor Rimpoche carried his Guru from Tibet to India, and no matter how many times I tell that story, it has profound meaning and value. It has a meaning beyond anything that could be determined conceptually, and it's one of those things where you never know when the memory of it is going to come up. Some people would say that carrying one's Guru from Tibet to India could never happen, or it was made up by others who weren't there, or that they were in shock or whatever it might be. But they *weren't* in shock and it *did* happen, and other things very similar to it happened as well.

There is the practice of short moments, repeated many times, and if you want to practice Guru devotion, you can. I had no idea how to practice Guru devotion. There were lots of books on it, but I thought, "Well, these are all practices that I don't do and I can't relate to." So instead, I just started thinking about my Guru and what he was doing that day. Devotion is a great teacher, because it brings to a complete stop the whole framework of intellectual pondering on different ideas. What it is replaced with is wisdom exaltation and sublime enlightened energy, and this is what we always are.

Rimpoche carrying Thuksey Rinpoche on his own back all the way from Tibet to India is an example of Guru devotion: short moments of Guru devotion, repeated many times, become spontaneous and automatic. The first day I met him he said, "This is the greatest accomplishment of my life." I was struck by that. I thought, "Hmm, I'm going to need to reflect on this, because it's so far beyond my comprehension." As I practiced Guru Yoga in my own way, I found myself thinking about Rimpoche more and more—and not just thinking—but loving him more and more each moment with a kind of love I'd never had before. There was complete love and trust. The more I fell deeply in love with Rimpoche, the more I fell deeply in love with everything and everyone. For me, it allowed perception to be totally pure and for suffering to completely end. Instead, love and trust, complete love and trust.

Guru Yoga begins as devotion to a Lineage teacher who has been requested to pass on the tradition. It has been specifically requested of me to pass on "furtherance of Dzogchen," so that Dzogchen can be understood by many people in this era—understood and realized. Because it is an unbroken Lineage, everything that is spoken sounds so similar to everything that has gone before.

I didn't set out to become a Lineage Holder or anything of that kind. I didn't set out to have ceremonies or embroidered robes or monasteries. The Tibetan way is very unlike the West; their way is subtle rather than direct. I did not hear directly from my Guru that I was named a Lineage Holder; I heard about it on the Internet! That's where my teacher made the statement. I had nothing to do with it. I never sought it, never dreamt of it and never had any idea of it whatsoever.

Right before I received this Teaching, I had something occur that is incredibly important in this Teaching, which is that I had a complete release from anything to do with the body-mind. It was just a complete release, and the body-mind just became another seldom thought-about data stream.

As a Guru has already realized open intelligence and what that is and lives as its spontaneous Transmission, by linking ourselves to the Guru we're able to get a taste of that. Linking to the Guru and devotion to the Guru initially can be a thought or a feeling, and it can be a simple practice like, "Every time I remember today, I'm going to think about the Guru and his many compassionate qualities and activities. I'm going to think about what he is doing today and how he is benefitting beings."

This is my own experience, and this is how I approached it. I thought, "Well, he's living in his cave," or he was at the time and, "He's meditating night and day," or other things like, "He's making sure that people have everything they need—blankets, coats, food. He is taking care of all the refugees, and his whole life is for the benefit of all." Through thoughts like that the heart opens up. The Tibetans say that the Guru lives in the heart, that open intelligence is in the heart, not between the ears—in the heart, a feeling in the heart.

When Wangdor Rimpoche died—that is, when he went on emanation vacation!—my relationship with him did not end, but in my own experience it did change in certain ways. Not only did I see that I would have many more responsibilities than I had thought I would have, but also all of a sudden I felt the ability to proceed—that I had everything needed to go forward. And as things develop, we will have everything needed to go forward. As I said, I see Rimpoche as being on an emanation vacation. We can't see him anymore, although actually we do see him, but he looks different! Rimpoche is right here; he's only on an emanation vacation.

We miss his physical emanation, but the power of what Rimpoche is is so far beyond any power we experienced of Rimpoche when he was alive. And this is the way he pushes us over the cliff again, as it were—showing us that he didn't go anywhere. Yes, an emanation vacation, but he's here clearer to me than he's ever been, and his presence and power of generosity are even more powerful.

Fourth Section

EMPOWERING ONE'S PRACTICE

THE DYNAMIC DISPLAY
CHAPTER EIGHTEEN

We are introduced to open intelligence and then we begin to practice, and the more we practice, the more we can just look at the river—this life—as it flows on by. We can look at the boulders, the currents and the waves, but we're standing on the bank of the river; we're not caught in the currents of the river. If we're caught *in* the river, well . . . So, we have that choice: to be caught in the violent currents of the river, or to stand peacefully on the banks of the river observing it as it passes.

Sometimes though we may be in a circumstance that is so intense that we are back in the river. To be back in the river doesn't matter—as long as we practice. "I'm back in the river, but I am showing up for myself completely and showing up for everyone by holding true to the practice." We might feel, "Gosh, I'm not aware. I don't even know what pure intelligence is. Where did it go?" but even those thoughts require open intelligence—there's no way to have thoughts like that without open intelligence. So see, there's no way out! There's no way to deny the aware quality of pure intelligence in any perception.

When we are caught up in a whirl of positive, negative and neutral thoughts and lots of emotions and sensations—and really believing that they are true—we just can't identify them for what they are, which is open intelligence, strong mind. But once we have the tools to identify it, then we can. Then the easeful surfing can take place, and the tsunami is no longer so threatening!

Everything has been so mixed up about what a human being actually is, and in defining ourselves in the reified ways that we have, we have limited ourselves. However, when we see everything as beneficial energy, that view subsumes all definitions within the comprehensive order of perfect knowledge. Then we are able to have the discernment and insight to look at all definitions and see whether they can be useful or not, and how the useful ones can be built on with perfect knowledge.

An example of instinctive recognition is to see that fear, anxiety and panic are pure as open intelligence, and that having extreme emotional states is absolutely pure, and that there is nothing that needs to be done about them. In fact, they will persist until they're recognized as pure. That's the way it is. There's no way of *contriving* a perception to make it pure. It is a matter of seeing the fundamental purity of whatever is arising as inseparable from open intelligence. This is the realization that will carry you through.

Our heart-truth is that we were born with the capacity for beneficial action, and all the other ways in which we have been trained have been grossly in error. The great fallacy of reification comes because everything has been mis-defined from the beginning. For instance, we have never been meant to worship our human life as superior to all other forms of life.

Even if you have all kinds of things going on and you suddenly went mad; nevertheless, open intelligence pervades all, and it would remain absolutely clear and present in that moment of madness. So really, there's nothing to fear. Even though there might be that one person in the world that people really like to fear these days, there's nothing to fear. That one person is an excellent opportunity for practice, no matter whom you think that one person is!

Potency=awareness, anxiety=awareness, other strong feelings=awareness. In holding to this view, everything becomes equal and even. Equalness and evenness=awareness. Awareness settles everything into gentle power, but it doesn't mean that it is a sappy kind of gentle power. "Woo-woo, oh, I have to be nice all the time." Rather, it's a complete and skilled response to every single circumstance.

A participant said once in a teaching that his biggest delusion was in thinking that he could control his data. Through our training in reification, we have indeed been trained to think that way: that we can control our data, and not only that, that we're expected to, and if we don't, we're a failure. That applies to everything: mental, emotional, spiritual and physical data. With the Four Mainstays we can support each other to normalize everything that's going on—together—and to speak up about what's going on, and see that we no longer need to control what is coming up for us.

When we are first introduced to open intelligence, the introduction calls upon something deep within us that we have been waiting for all of our lives. We have been searching. In every single thing we have looked at, in every person we have met, we have been wanting them to somehow confirm what is already present in us, but which has remained hidden. We are calling upon every circumstance or person we see or meet to affirm that enlightenment is real, but just not knowing that this is what we were actually looking for.

The yearning for love that we so intensely feel is actually a yearning for open intelligence, for strong mind. The romance and intimacy we want is actually a wish for intimacy with open intelligence and love. When we're introduced to open intelligence, it is an affirmation of what we've always known to be true.

Throughout life there have been things that we have thought about ourselves, and especially many negative things. But the highs can be an issue too, and the highs can go from just thinking "I feel really good today," all the way to, "I feel like I am enlightened," or to a level of mania where we are buying up the store each night on Amazon! I can see that some people might be able to relate to this! That's good. It's good to know about what life is like, not only for us but for everyone. What is more, it's so good to hear what life *really* is—loving open intelligence.

TO RESOLVE AGGRESSION

It could be that suddenly we may take a nosedive into a data stream, like for instance into aggression. There are plenty of opportunities for aggression. It could be self-aggression or aggression outwards towards others. Aggression is very sneaky, because things like self-aggression can be very subtle. "I'm not good enough; I'm not pretty enough; I'm not practicing awareness enough. I don't really know what awareness is. I don't

167

think I'm good enough for a career or a family," or whatever it might be. This is self-aggression.

The way to be with this is to instinctively recognize it as the dynamic energy of open intelligence. This is more soothing than any kind of antidote we could apply to the self-aggression. To instinctively recognize open intelligence moment-to-moment for greater and greater durations is similar to experiencing the warmth of the sun. Instead of just *thinking* about the sun and how it does this and that, we're actually *experiencing* the sun!

Just let everything be *as it is*, and everything reveals itself *as it is* more and more obviously. There's nothing to be afraid of and nothing to hope for really. Each moment is brand new, and there isn't a single person who knows what the next moment will bring, and this is so for all beings.

Even the TV or movies or news programs can be great teachers if one maintains pure perception. With some of the characters appearing on the news and otherwise in the media, things can get us very riled up. However, from pure perception all we see is the dynamic energy of awareness.

To go on to instinctive recognition, and especially to pure perception, requires that we be completely naked. With all of the energies and tensions that have built up and which have led to our behavior today, we allow all of them to completely be as they are. When we are once again in a situation where there is a tendency to feel that we are wrong, bad or at fault, we'll get an opportunity to see how we are doing with that challenge. Without a need to teach ourselves anything or to teach others anything or to make pronouncements about where we're at, we can just be naked and open and available.

By seeing the reality of, for instance, hatred *as it is*—which is the reality of great benefit, very great perfect love—it ends our ability to ever hate anyone. It enables us to have only perfect love and to be able to share perfect love with everyone. This is inexhaustible perfect love, and not love that we're going to experience just for a little while when we feel like it, which then goes away. This is love forever and for everyone and everything.

I can say at my ripe age that what you have chosen for yourself, this devotion to the practice, is the only way to be. What you have chosen for yourself guarantees that love will never be absent in your life, and love will not be absent at the time of so-called death.

YOUR MOTIVATION AND INTENTION

I was asked once about how to overcome the fear about being committed to this practice. Well, I can liken it to an investment. Do you want to invest your money in something that you know will be an abysmal failure, or do you want to invest in something that is going to give incredible benefits every single minute and is certain to succeed? Once that decision is made, a certain kind of rigor is required.

We already commit lots of rigorous vitality to all kinds of things in life, and we are devoted to many things in our life, so we already know what devotion is, even if we never called it "devotion." It's not foreign to any of us; but now we just consolidate it. "Instead of tussling with data, I'm going to focus my devotion in a resolute way, so that it's forever more held within the context of enlivening energy." Your motivation and intention need to be clear, and for each of us the way that this is directed can be something different.

There's no way to find bodily security through any means; there's no way to find security of the emotions and the mind through any means. No amount of money can give that kind of ease; no kind of physical setting can give that kind of ease. The only reality of that ease is the power of great benefit, and from that vantage we are able to settle into the reality of who we are in all circumstances. We settle into the best of who we are. We settle into the fulfillment of a dream we may not know we have. There's no need to get there. There's no "right here" and "far away," and there's nothing in between.

It is generally easier to be with those who share our open-intelligence view; however, when we're with people who don't share that view, we can be responsive to whatever is needed. For example, I might go to the grocery store and on the way I pass all kinds of people. I might see homeless people or I might see the usual members of the local community or new members of the community, and with each one there is a response according to time, place and circumstance.

I'm not there to preach; I'm simply there saying hello or responding to whatever is requested, so to speak, from the other person. I might see someone who is all wrapped up in emotion, and I can just be there with them. It doesn't matter what they say or what they do, I feel a deep connection. I'm not saying this is a special thing about me; what I'm portraying is part of the realization of open-intelligence reality that's true for everyone.

"To deeply love the work we do" doesn't mean getting a job we don't like and then trying to love it deeply! It means knowing what we love and then finding that kind of work or service, and because we already love it, we will increasingly love it deeply. We look within and we decide on what we love deeply, and then we practice the way of benefit deeply in the world. In being able to know our strengths, gifts and talents, we are brought into liveliness, where we don't really have to think about whether or not we love the work. Work and play become the same, and there is no difference between them.

National boundaries are failing and cultures are becoming globalized. We're more and more being introduced to living as part of one global culture. Gradually the national boundaries will fail, not because of wars between countries or other types of predicaments, but more because it is what people really want. Maybe not all politicians want this, but politicians too will need to adapt. The best way we can prepare ourselves for the future and prepare our children is through strong mind. Without strong mind, we cannot be strong leaders in our community, and we can't be strong leaders generally.

Each person individually has a knowledge base to share. It may not be in the context of whatever career we had when we first started out, as we probably will shift priorities according to how we can be of greatest benefit to all. Some people will contribute globally, others locally. That's just the way it is. There isn't any "better" type of knowledge or contribution.

More and more we are a global co-operative society, and even though the media outlets describe all kinds of horror, that is only one interpretation of things. It's important to realize that many people around the world don't watch the same sort of news reporting that we watch. If we don't focus solely on our own version of the news, what we can see is that many, many people have a very different vantage from ours about what is happening in the world.

I really feel that it's important for a culture to accept responsibility for evolution and for the fact that *we're in charge* of this evolutionary leap. We can take responsibility for it. We can talk about it in simple terms that make sense to everyone. We are going through a tremendous evolution right now where human beings are coming to see who they truly are. Another example from earlier evolution was when someone suddenly had the thought, "Maybe I don't need to walk around on all fours any longer. I think I'll just try to stand up on two legs!" That was a huge leap.

Almost everyone has been operating under the premise of a lie, a lie that we have been trained in so that we can fit into all the reified political and economic activities of the world. Human beings have developed in this way, but now it's time for human beings to live as they actually are. This is really a good way to look at it. "Well, I've been lying to myself, and now I know who I am, so I'm going to devote my whole life to that reality."

It's a good plan, don't you think! We as human beings need to seize the capabilities that are *ours*. This is the way evolution or significant change has always worked, whether it was coming to stand on two feet or learning to read and write. We seized these enthusiastically because they were major innovations that could be used by many people.

Currently, enlightened open intelligence is unintelligible to most people; however, through innovative educational technologies, exponentially greater numbers of beings will enjoy enlightened open intelligence, until we reach the point where primitive intelligence will no longer be predominant. This is an evolutionary leap. Until the leap is complete, there will be sublime beings, practitioners and ordinary beings.

THE FOUR PRACTICES FOR SUBLIME PRACTITIONERS

There are four practices of what are considered sublime practitioners, and they are *indescribability, openness, spontaneous presence* and *indivisibility*. These four—indescribability, openness, spontaneous presence and indivisibility—are really the only practices one needs to have when one has reached the point of not needing to take short moments any longer.

Indescribability, or ineffability, refers primarily to primordial purity, to what is primordially pure from the very beginning. It is alert and aware and also profoundly intelligent. Like the sun emanates its rays, open intelligence emanates the warm rays of profound wisdom and compassion, the power to benefit all and the power to enlighten the collective. All of this is emanating non-stop; there's no on/off switch. It's an inexhaustible outpouring of profound wisdom, compassion and skillful means for the benefit of all.

Everything is just going along and data aren't troublesome, and so openness is a spontaneously flowing emanation. The more committed we are in a natural way from our heart, the more openness there is. It may not be in every situation or all the time as yet, but it will be. However, it doesn't mean that openness will look a certain way, like, "Oh, I'm so open. I love everybody. Everyone is just great!"

Openness means complete openness to everyone and everything, so it is a matter of knowing what's going on with everybody. For instance, you can just look around a room, take a glance at everybody and you kind of know where they're coming from. It's very powerful, because it's essential in terms of considering issues with people and then coming to some kind of conclusion together.

Spontaneous presence. Without any effort, without anything needing to be done, open intelligence is spontaneously present. That's really all there is to say about it—spontaneous presence. There is no longer an urge to try to grab for it or get it or do anything at all, as open intelligence is spontaneously present.

All of these—the ineffability, the openness, the spontaneous presence and the indivisibility—are indivisible and inseparable. They're not individual things like, "Oh, here's my box for ineffability, I'll put that in there. Over here, openness, we'll put that in there." Indescribability, openness, spontaneous presence and indivisibility—you could say that they are the ultimate practice that is indivisible from the Four Mainstays. They are the hidden practice in the Four Mainstays, because through the Four Mainstays all of these will become clear.

SOMETHING SO MUCH GREATER THAN OUR REIFIED SELF

CHAPTER NINETEEN

When I first had the nature of mind clarified for me, the only word that came to my mind was *immaculate*. I couldn't think of anything else to relate it to—not any kind of conceptual framework I had ever heard, whether mystical, esoteric, religious or philosophical—nothing. Immaculate.

Please take these instructions to heart, and if you haven't begun practicing short moments, please do. Rely on the people in the resting community. No matter who you are, rely on the people in the community. I rely on the people in the community, and I enjoy it a great deal!

The most definitive thing we can say about intelligence is that there is either pure intelligence, or, a reified intelligence that isn't felt to be pure. One or the other, that's it.

Usually when individuals are first introduced to open intelligence, there is an immediate fear that the felt presence of open intelligence will go away, because this has been our experience—trying to rely on something and then feeling that it goes away. When fear comes up, rest. Rest. Keep resting and you'll come to see that the fear itself is the power of wisdom. That's what it really is; it has just been misnamed.

We find that with the practice of short moments, repeated many times, more and more open intelligence becomes obvious and spontaneous to us. There really is no recognition or realization of emptiness until there is spontaneous great bliss seeing emptiness. Spontaneous great bliss and emptiness are indivisible and inseparable. There is no understanding and realizing spontaneous great bliss unless it is seeing emptiness.

Spontaneous great bliss seeing emptiness is really worth practicing—very much worth practicing. Short moments until continuous. Words like "ecstasy" and "exaltation" when used in this context also give us a sense of something so much greater than our reified self. We can enter into it easily, because it's actually what we have always been and have always been looking for.

If you're a newcomer to this practice, I would suggest practicing short moments every day. It doesn't matter whether on the first day it's one time of short moments, or the next day three times, or whatever it may be. Maybe the first day it's no times, and then on the second day you remember once, "Oh yeah, I'm supposed to be practicing short moments," and then you pick it up. It could also be anywhere within a range from nothing up to every single minute of the day. Short moments become longer and longer, and then one day all of a sudden you notice that everything is an even flow, and short moments aren't required any longer.

Each short moment of open intelligence is self-kept. That means that it never goes away; it is self-kept. It is experienced and realized. It's like putting $100 into your bank account, and you keep putting more in and never taking any out. The quantity keeps building and building and increasing in potency. Same thing with short moments; the power increases exponentially without a need to examine it and try to explain it or put it into words.

Before it is possible to have a good sense of instinctive recognition of open intelligence, it usually requires coming to a deep understanding that open intelligence is actually already the case. It starts with a profound interest in open intelligence and then a deepening understanding of it through listening to talks and reading the texts and really grokking them. "Yes, I know what open intelligence is and I'm fully prepared to practice it."

That's the next step—practice. "Practicing" means the instinctive recognition of open intelligence for short moments, many times. So, rather than just thinking about open intelligence, through the short moments practice, now we have an instinctive sense of open intelligence knowing itself. Moment-to-moment we bring this about as often as we remember to do so.

We might hear something that at first makes very little sense or even no sense, like for example the statement, "Mind is the vast expanse." Now, most of the time when people hear something like that, they don't really know what it means; in fact, they may have no idea at all. But at some point it becomes totally obvious what that means. It just comes to be! And that's the way it should be in order to maturely settle in.

SELF-SOOTHING

Getting completely lost in emotional states is just something that needs to be reined in, and when I say "rein it in," I mean immediately! It doesn't matter what the state is, short moments is the solution, and everything that can come up is included in that solution. Even if one is lost in an emotional state, it's impossible for that emotional state to persist finally. That's just the way it is; these states cannot persist, and eventually they're all gone, completely gone. So, one could say that one form of surfing the tsunami is simply trusting this, and relying on the experience that even the worst negative states eventually resolve and pass away.

Let's say that something like intense anger comes up. It is important to know that the anger is nothing other than open intelligence—emptiness—and everything that that is. However, before we reach that point of realization, from the vantage of reification the label of "anger" is primary, and emptiness is secondary. So, when someone is going through an intense emotional state, in that circumstance the emotion may be primary, and the emptiness is secondary. However, what is discovered through the practice is that *the emptiness is always primary*; the great bliss that is the reality of everything is already primary.

When we realize the reality of everything, it's a complete switch all at once. There is a soothing of one's life and being. Why is that? Because we have acknowledged who we are, and that acknowledgement is very soothing. It is just like with a child when the child is just going wild about something. There's no way to support the child through that unless there is acknowledgement of where the child is, so to speak, and showing them the support of soothing and also self-soothing. That is what the child needs in the end, and gradually children learn to self-soothe.

We as adults are actually doing exactly the same thing, because with short moments we learn to self-soothe. We're self-soothing, and not only that, we're with other people in a worldwide community who are doing the same thing through acknowledging their true being. The more we acknowledge our being and rest as that, the better things are for us. We allow this for ourselves through deep understanding of the Teaching, being able to see everything *as it is* and letting everything spontaneously release. When we're skilled at that, we can really handle whatever is coming up and see everything *as it is*.

Once we are more familiar with leaving a data stream *as it is*, pure perception is next—seeing everything as pure. As we acknowledge ourselves as a sublime being, we begin to see more and more that our entire environment, all data, are a sublime mandala, a pure mandala. This is what spontaneous presence is— the spontaneous presence of buddha in every moment. In every short moment, we are resting as a short moment of complete buddha-hood. "Buddha" is not a person or a thing; buddha is qualities and activities. Everything is the vast expanse of buddha—of buddha body, speech and mind. There is no other identity findable, so why not relax into the only identity that is truly findable? Take your openness all the way into the vast expanse of buddha; that's what I would suggest.

Without the limiting concepts of "self" and "other," there is just immense power for the enlightenment of all. We no longer need to examine things in the context of, "I am this particular person, and those over there are different from me," or, "This one and that one I like, but the other ones I don't like so much. If I were a better person then I'd be able to do this thing I want to do, but I'm not, so I think I'll go wallow in my self-pity and sit on the pity-pot for a while!" Now this is common to everyone, and the "pity-pot," so to speak, is a data stream that holds on for a bit and causes us to feel sorry for ourselves. Eventually the data stream disappears, but while it lasts it can be a very harsh obscuration of the display of our gifts.

One of the key points of the Teaching is the spontaneous self-release of data and freedom in immediate perception, complete perceptual openness in all experience. If we just sit for five minutes and observe, we can see how each of the arising data streams spontaneously self-release. It's impossible to hold on to a thought for more than an instant. Even if we go back and try to hold on to the thought, it's impossible. So, any idea that there is a train of thought or a string of thought—there is no such thing. This is the point of freedom in immediate perception: we relax, we see a thought come up and we see how quickly it releases on its own. Then it arises again and it releases, over and over again. It is emptiness taking itself to emptiness; there is no-thing in there anywhere. Data are the mind of great bliss seeing emptiness.

The reification of the three times—past, present and future—is like drawings in the sky. There's no past, present and future, and everything happens in a continuous flow, where there's no longer reference to past, present and future.

QUALITIES AND ACTIVITIES

Buddha-hood is shown by qualities and activities of mind, speech and body. Now, usually when we think about mind, speech, body, qualities and activities, we think of our skin suit. "Here's my body, my skin suit, and I'm inside it, and this is the location of my mind, body, speech, qualities and activities." However, open intelligence pervaded by love is a vast expanse, and *that* is our true mind and body. You see, we learn one thing about body and mind, but there's more to learn, more to directly realize.

Wisdom isn't something that we fetch intellectually, emotionally or physically or in any other way. It isn't something that's gotten. It already is, and so it's simply realized. The wisdom is enlightened mind. The more profound our seeing of the mind of great bliss seeing emptiness, the more settled, the more rested and the stronger that wisdom is.

The empowered and extraordinary skillful means of enlightened qualities and activities are always pouring forth from the heart. And I don't mean a single heart in a person, but the heart *as it is,* the Great Heart. The Great Heart automatically has empowered qualities and activities, and all of these are already ripened and liberated within you.

Empowered and extraordinary skillful means are qualities and activities of enlightened being. There isn't a certain package of enlightened qualities and activities and we only have what's in that package. Instead, we have inexhaustible qualities and activities of enlightened being.

DATA AS A TEACHER AND A FRIEND

With a proper introduction to open intelligence it's realized that data are the shining dynamic energy of open intelligence; however, it may take a while for that to become completely obvious. We have been trained to pay attention to thoughts, emotions and experiences, and as a result the reification of data has been foremost. The beginning phase, the introduction to open intelligence, is called deep understanding—realizing what is going on and then settling into a reality that is brand new.

The truth of reality is something we've always already known, but it just hasn't had a light shone on it. This is what my Gurus have done for me: they shine a bright light on the truth of reality, and it's up to me whether I want to get what they're saying and really live a life based on what they have offered me. So, it's cooperative, it's collaborative.

To recognize data as the dynamic energy of open intelligence is usually something that is completely new to us, so seen in that way one could say that data are appearing as a teacher at first. But at a certain point, data become more like a friend than a teacher. In instinctive recognition, open intelligence becomes more alive, and data are seen as a friend. We may initially try to use open intelligence as an antidote to "our friend" if it is acting up!

Our friend, the data, comes to us—in the form of anger, pride, envy, desire, hope, fear or whatever it might be—and we say, "Oh gosh, there you are. I know that you're really open intelligence, but I'm not sure exactly how to handle it. So, I'll just proceed as the teacher has instructed—to practice short moments of open intelligence, and allowing data to be as they are."

There is no need to try to be like everybody else who's living a life filled with data streams. If one hangs out with that type of community, then that is what one learns; that is the takeaway from any involvement in ordinary life. It's a matter of how we want to be in society. When people operate only from data streams, that is the context and extent of what they can see. They do not know that there is a permanent way to soothe the mind, a permanent way to have happiness—a *life* of happiness as well as a *death* of happiness. It just simply is not known; it's inconceivable, and that is why it is not recognized.

One of the great freedoms and advantages is to be able to have the time to practice the dharma. No one here has to work every minute of the day collecting roots just to get something to eat. Instead, we are all here at this Teaching and don't have to worry about where our food will be coming from. Each of us has at least enough money to be here today, and we have the advantage of having sufficient free time to prioritize the Teaching. And yet, I know there are people collecting roots somewhere who have significant realization and are in fact Dzogchen masters. Practicing and realizing don't have to do with whether one needs to be out collecting roots or not.

We may feel self-protective and defensive because we fear that we'll be abandoned by a person with whom we are in a relationship, even though they say that they're going to stick with us. But will they really? Well, no one knows. Everything is totally impermanent. So, no matter where we are and who we're in a relationship with, our practice of impermanence won't ever change.

For quite a few people, for whatever reason, strong emotions can come up; however, strong emotions are equal to wisdom. This is the most important aspect to remember about strong emotions— to identify their co-equal wisdom, rather than rushing to examine them from a Freudian perspective or some other perspective that we have learned. Once again, surfing the tsunami, surfing the tsunami . . .

A feeling is only the desire for experience. Remember that. Do you want to go into that experience, or do you want to continue to open up to whatever is available in resting as open intelligence? In opening up to strong mind, you can see that not only is joy brought to your life, but many other freedoms and advantages as well. It's important to look back in retrospect to compare before-and-after to really see what the results are in your own life. For each individual, the realization is the same, exactly the same, yet each has a certain flavor, a certain taste.

What other virtue is comparable to that of bringing an end to the delusion of everything having an independent material reality? Materiality—establishing things in terms of the material reality of everything—has been of great importance in the world. However, even with the forging ahead of that attitude of materiality, at the same time there are many individuals who are committed to looking at things in an entirely different way, and we can already see that coming about in society.

No matter how brilliant people are within the context of reification—inventing all kinds of fantastic devices and doing inconceivable types of things—enlightenment is more powerful than all of this. So, I always ask, "Well, if all these incredible things can be done without enlightenment, what would happen *with* the gift of enlightenment?"

I have a good friend who is a doctor, and I once asked him, "What do you do with all the heaviness that comes with seeing people suffering and experiencing death so much." He replied, "When I leave one patient's room, while I'm walking to the next room, I relax completely. I want to be an open vehicle for the person I'm seeing. I want them to feel that I really care and that I'm not thinking about other things while I'm treating them." He is such a beautiful being. Living-buddhas come in many forms, and some come to enlighten all beings, but others come as, say, a doctor who is a loving vehicle for the patients they are seeing.

BE GENTLE WITH YOURSELF

CHAPTER TWENTY

From my Guru I learned that intelligence and love is all that is. "Intelligence" isn't something that is stark and without feeling; what we are in our essence is *loving* open intelligence. Love also means compassion, but not a contrived compassion that we need to cultivate or effort for. Instead, resting completely as our natural state of being, without any need to make or do anything, we remain as we are.

We're not trying to get to anything or get away from anything. Everything, no matter what it is, is at ease. We have learned through reification that life is filled with victory and upset, with the two opposite poles of striving for victory and happiness and pushing away defeat and upset. But in resting we find that everything is open intelligence, everything is love, with no need to strive for victory or push away defeat.

If someone gives you something of great value, something that can bring you to enlightenment in this very life, you would not let it go. If you have been given the wish-fulfilling jewel, you would be careful not to lose it.

There is a story about a poor woman who lives in a world of gold, but because she doesn't recognize the value of gold, she is convinced that she is poor. Using this simple story as an illustration, if we don't recognize open intelligence, we spend our life emphasizing the impoverished prison of data reification, rather than the rich powers of great benefit. However, when we rely on open intelligence, we recognize the gold that is the foundation and substance of all of reality. All data shine forth as the golden luminosity of pure intelligence. In a world of gold, everything is gold.

Any reified solution to the world's problems is rooted in impermanence, so I don't want to work on something impermanent myself. I am interested in developing what is permanent, and Wangdor Rimpoche instructed us to do this. Not only instructed us, but he said, we *will* do it! Enlightenment for all right now is what I want to work on.

"Competition within oneself" means to always be fighting with this thought, that emotion, that experience. "Oh, I can't have this thought, I can't have that emotion or I'm a bad person. I better have only these other thoughts. Am I better than that other person?" Does that sound relaxed? We're meant to be relaxed and free. We are meant to be easeful, relaxed and free, and we have the opportunity through the practice of short moments to be open to the radiant wisdom of open intelligence, which will carry us through any tsunami.

This is easy to see in watching very small children who are relaxed and free. Everything they learn about thoughts and emotions and competition is pretty much pasted upon them by their family, caregivers, teachers and the world around them. Life is not a competition; it's all-inclusive. It doesn't matter what forms something takes or whether it is described as good or bad, its light-energy of radiance isn't lessened.

We all want happiness, but there's no such thing as personal happiness. How could we figure out where personal happiness is when everything is not and not-not? We could think about "not and not-not" for the rest of our lives and never figure it out. "Figuring things out" is not what is taught here!

A so-called individual does not have an independent nature separate or apart from the pure benefit feed. The inconceivable space of pure benefit is always present within both general and individual data streams, whether recognized or not. The traveler always already lives as the destination of pure benefit; thus, seeking to be a good person through reified means does not reveal the profound meaning of human life. It is like shooting an arrow in the dark. The pure benefit feed, ever radiant, is the deathless, permanent, sublime reality of everything and everyone and is present without any effort at all.

The focus needs to shift from being exclusively fixed on oneself, as in, "My way of being and all of my actions need to be loved." With the practice, instead of the wish being, "I need to be loved and I want someone to love me," the question becomes, "What can I give? How can I love? How can I love my Guru? How can I love everyone else?" By loving the Guru unconditionally—even though some people bristle at that idea—that is the door to walk through to love everyone unconditionally. It's a very important instruction.

We're not to blame for reification, because this is the way we have been trained all of our lives. Gradually we have learned to be a separate self, but what a lonely, isolated place to be—a hut of self-concern and reification. Yet, at the same time there is no better place to be, because it is also the seat of the wish-fulfilling jewel of open intelligence. Each person is the treasure box with the wish-fulfilling jewel inside.

We have all been trained in a society based on discipline-and-punish. This comes about through the religious philosophies that imply that there's something wrong with us. Most people, even if they consider themselves atheist or agnostic, are affected by this all day, every day. What this means is that people look down on themselves and don't like themselves. They feel that they are marked by original sin or karma and that they can't progress outside of that context. I'm sure everyone can relate to what I'm saying. I know that I certainly can.

In a society based on the idea that people are original sinners or bound by karma, all of life is spent trying to be good, trying to be better, trying to have a better self-image. In the context of discipline-and-punish this is considered to be the only way that people can live a happy life. In the world of discipline-and-punish, we grow to feel that we don't deserve what is good. As we can see, it's a battle; not only does society discipline us as individuals, we discipline ourselves continuously.

Out of this religious philosophy grew the economic system of capitalism, and within capitalism discipline-and-punish is the way things are done. In companies employees are disciplined, and then if they veer from whatever their position description is, they are punished in some way. This is so much a part of human society today, and to hear it talked about in a direct way is really shocking. It's really shocking to hear that our lifestyle has been and is now discipline-and-punish.

We have a heavy under-mutter of this type of reification about what a human being is and is not. We are constantly faced with this, but in Dzogchen practice we have a way to end the process of discipline-and-punish. We have a way of bringing great bliss seeing emptiness into our lives. We find a whole new type of human intelligence, but not something that is esoteric. It's simply the way human beings are: we are open intelligence and love. That is our actual nature, and the culture of discipline-and-punish can be outshone in every single instant. This is the reason why when we are introduced to open intelligence, we feel such a tremendous relief, because it outshines the whole process of discipline-and-punish. We open up to expansive open intelligence and love.

I raised my two children with no philosophy of discipline-or-punish, and it had a very profound effect on them, and they passed this on to their families as well. Bye, bye discipline-and-punish! One of the important aspects of community is that we support one another to live outside of the realm of discipline-and-punish. We love each other, and it's obvious, not only to us, but also to many people that we really love each other and that we love the community in which we live.

THE FOCUS ON OUR OWN FEELINGS

Generally, Western cultures place value on focusing on personal feelings more than the energy of the people and situations around us. What is the consequence of this way of relating to our emotions? First, it can cause us to be extremely sensitive. We react emotionally to almost everything and everyone around us. What is the problem with connecting our identity or ego, our very sense of self, with our emotional state of mind? Emotions become the core of our identity, and almost literally we are what we feel because we have identified directly with the emotions. The English language expresses this idea, saying, "I *am* angry," rather than "I *have* anger" as they do in other languages. In the Tibetan language one actually says, "Anger is present" and does not connect the emotion with "I" at all.

It's also true in our culture that people are going everywhere to *every* kind of possible antidote that could possibly be used. Any kind of curative fantasy will be found and used! Each individual finds and uses their own way of being in the world, whether they're a criminal or a great buddha or saint. Every person chooses the way they're going to live their life.

One of the biggest drawbacks for people is self-contempt. Even if it comes out as arrogance, it is still self-contempt—not feeling secure enough in oneself to speak from open intelligence, and maybe even thinking, "I don't deserve to be enlightened, or I will never be enlightened." Who cares what the thought is? So, again, quantity of short moments, not quality, because there is no way to describe it in terms of qualities. I don't try. It just is as it is, whatever it is.

When we have a twinge of emotion and we rest, we get a huge return on our investment, as it were. Everyone is at least sort of interested in finances, so, here we are: when something comes up and there's that twinge of emotion—but instead we rest—then we get the return on the investment of open intelligence. If we go off into a story about the twinge, then we reinforce our data streams, and the return on that investment is just more reification.

Maybe you're talking with someone and they're just going on and on obsessively about something. Have you ever had that happen? You may have an important appointment, and they're still going on and on with not a clue about what you might be up to. "Oh, am I going to make it to my appointment? Will this person ever shut-up?" All of these thoughts are born of a brewing anxiety and anger that we don't know what to do with, but yet we're presented with it all of the time.

By resting as loving open intelligence, instead of just getting frantic, we can see the solution to that situation. Whether it is feeling frantic, anxious, angry, upset or whatever, until we learn to identify it as open intelligence we don't really have a deep understanding of what's going on. However, by resting totally, deeply and completely, we know exactly what to do and how to act. We can see clearly what the solution is in any situation. Each circumstance has its own wisdom and discernment.

Especially with women it is very common to be very hard on oneself. Whatever the circumstances, the practice is short moments, many times, little by little, right? That's what I would say: little by little. That doesn't mean necessarily that the under-muttering goes away completely, but what it does mean is that the recognition comes that we're already enlightened, and we more and more realize enlightenment. That's what the word "realization" means: we real-ize enlightenment, we *make it real*. It's a big leap. We have been taught all of our lives something so entirely different, but, hey, I know quite a few who have made the leap!

What is perfect knowledge, and does "having perfect knowledge" mean I have to get a larger library to contain all my books? No. Perfect knowledge means recognizing that data are in fact the dynamic energy of open intelligence. By not insisting that data have some kind of dictionary definition that needs to be fussed over, data come to be seen as spontaneously perfect knowledge, which provides insight and discernment in how to act in time, place and circumstance. Each place and circumstance demands a certain response, and that responsiveness can come from one of two domains: from reification or from perfect knowledge.

After the recognition of enlightenment, the only activity that can be thought of is the enlightenment of all, right now. The life of benefit and the benefit of all beings can be the only purpose of life. All personal aims have been totally accomplished; there isn't anything else to accomplish, nothing at all. If life ended right now, there would be complete accomplishment of all goals, because there's nothing else to attain.

In reflecting back on life, we can see that every single moment has been some kind of moment of furthering an accomplishment, and so it may seem inconceivable to realize that all personal aims have been attained and that there is nothing left to do. To see this clearly is the complete release from a life of constant accomplishment.

There might be some sort of strong afflictive state that feels totally gripping, even to the point that it is overwhelming, like you're being choked to death. If you haven't had such a mental state, I pray that you do! I pray that you have extreme mental states that physically take you over, because *the greater the affliction, the greater the realization*!

To say, "I am panicked and overwhelmed. I can't take it; this is unbearable and I want to get rid of it," is the best way to keep a mental state! Instead, whatever the afflictive state is, let it be *as it is*. If people you know are undergoing an extreme mental state, support them to see it *as it is*. Don't support them to see some kind of whacky, revised version of reality, reinforcing things in them about money, relationships, or whatever it might be. This is by far the best way to support them—and yourself.

The Four Mainstays are essential to the Teaching. The Four Mainstays provide us with a community where we can see the actual results of realization come forth in everyone. By seeing the realization come forth in everyone, we can realize it in ourselves. By having community, we can enter into the beneficial lifestyle associated with that community. If we're in community, then I would say there's less of an opportunity of backsliding, because we are with a large group of people who have the same commitment—which is that all should realize their greatest possibility—and each supports the other in that way.

We have a firm foundation through the Four Mainstays, and we have through that everything that we need. We have teachers, we have media, we have the practice of short moments, we have a worldwide community. All of the Four Mainstays together provide a go-to foundation.

I always reflect every single day on the incredible beauty of the community of practitioners in this Teaching. I'm thinking about you all the time! To me it's just the most marvelous manifestation to see all of you. It's just totally incredible. I respect you, and I thank you for taking this on as an example to everyone. I am so grateful for your presence in the world.

In community we each do our part. Whatever it is we're contributing, that's what we contribute. I thank all of you who have participated and are participating, I know each person has contributed fully in their own way. I am very grateful to be with you, and I appreciate each one of you exactly as you are. This is what we all give each other: we appreciate each one exactly as they are. It's not like, "Oh, here comes that one again; I need to try my best to appreciate them." It isn't a contrived practice. Just simply by resting, relaxing and relying on open intelligence, we see what magic can happen!

I was once in the hospital, and I had tubes in my arm and those little hanging bags dripping medicine into my body. I was on a wing of the hospital where there were a lot of very sick people, people who were much sicker than I was, and I would be lying there and I would pray for the people. I would pray that they be able to see themselves as they are, so that they don't have to live only in sickness and misery. That has been a practice of mine for a long time.

At my age of seventy-four, I can say I am so happy I have lived as I did. I'm so happy I didn't turn back, turn away or give up. For me, to be quite honest, I couldn't, because I knew that if I did turn away, it would mean insanity or death, one of the two. I really felt that way. I felt that if I held to a life of reification, it would be a life of constant swinging on the gates of insanity and death as my only opportunity. At seventy-four I'm free to be, and I understand the symbology of perpetual or eternal youth, because I feel that way!

THE POWER OF ONE SIMPLE CHANGE

Many of us spend our whole life as if on trial for our data streams. It's as if we were sitting in the witness stand, and we look out and see that we are also the prosecutor, the defense attorney, the judge and the jury all at once! However, it's not necessary to continually be interrogating ourselves about everything we have said and done. We have learned over the years to focus on these data streams and identify with them, but by doing so, we've kept ourselves in a prison.

Yet, there's no need to worry. We have always been completely exonerated, because none of the data about which we've been questioning ourselves have an independent nature. When we simply rely on open intelligence for short moments, repeated many times, this becomes obvious. Blaming ourselves, hating ourselves, demeaning ourselves may have been the prison we have kept ourselves in, but we now have a way out.

The essence of your own being doesn't need anything to prop it up; it simply is, so relax and enjoy! Please don't be mean to yourself any longer. I really ask you this from my heart.

We may all have had thoughts come up like, "Oh, will I ever be happy? Will I ever be able to overcome the things that have always bothered me? Will I ever be able to get over the things that people have done to me?" Know that it's possible to rely on open intelligence whatever the appearance might be. Don't ever settle for any label about anything. To hold to any idea like, "This is the way it has always been, and this is the way it is going to be from now on," is so totally limiting. When we rely on the natural ease of being, we discover that every single moment is the supreme moment of complete spaciousness that has never been tied to anything. It's completely pure, entirely restful, and is filled with an energy beyond anything that can ever be cooked up through data.

Another way of describing this is to say that when we rest, we are resting as love. Love is already within us; it's what we really are, and this connects us with everyone and everything. In love there is no separation, and it's in this love that there is a haven of complete and immense safety and comfort. From the beginning of our lives we've looked for safety, comfort and love from our caregivers, our homes and outer circumstances, but we were never really able to find safety or comfort that we could ultimately count on. Pretty soon we started to look to other places, like romance, food, money, work and so on, but the safety and comfort somehow always escaped our grasp.

Through relying on open intelligence we discover that the nature of our own being is the absolute safety and absolute love that we've been seeking. Until we rest in that basis, life will be fraught with uncertainty. No matter where we are searching, unless we know this underlying basis that is the utterly safe haven of rest, we just can't find a truly safe place anywhere.

I would ask you to be gentle with yourself and others. You can be with others in this gentle way, because you've learned what makes them tick. And how did you learn that? Because you have seen clearly what makes *you* tick, and by knowing that, you can truly know yourself and others. Open intelligence overcomes all negativity with the balanced view of wisdom.

This means that your primary relationship with everyone is from the self-perfect nature of open intelligence, because through relying on open intelligence you've come to see that you and everyone else is part of the natural order of everything. To realize this does not require exertion. Everything is completely at ease, no matter what it is. Know this, and please be gentle with yourself. Please give to yourself and to all others the greatest gift you can give.

Whatever we are looking for anywhere else, it already exists within us. It's by relying on open intelligence repeatedly, for short moments, many times, over and over again, that we gain familiarity with it, and we find the real safety and comfort we've always been looking for. When surfing a tsunami, this will carry you through.

PITH INSTRUCTIONS
CHAPTER TWENTY-ONE

There are short, pithy teachings that are so powerful that, with just a few of them, you could practice for the rest of your life.

The first time that there is an instinctive realization of a pith instruction—rather than merely an intellectual understanding—it is extremely profound.

The enlightenment of all is always already accomplished.

Open intelligence is where all the reified data of negative and positive are complete—free from accepting and rejecting.

There are no individual beings anywhere.

We must be free from self-cherishing individualism and motivated by enlightenment for all.

Data cannot be controlled, only outshone spontaneously.

It is not that strong mind has no emotions or feelings. Rather, the emotions and the thoughts are *not ordinary*; they are a display of wisdom.

Many fixate on what is not real as real, so that it certainly seems real. They fixate on confusion where there is no confusion, so that there certainly seems to be confusion.

Seeking to avoid pain, many run headlong into suffering. Even though beings long for happiness, they foolishly destroy it as if it were the enemy.

In short moments, repeated many times, open intelligence becomes obvious at all times. Short moments, many times is the meditation of Dzogchen.

Whatever you believe about yourself, that is what you will seem to be.

Many are deceived by misconstruing what is not so as so, and ordinary mind is seduced by trivial reification in all its variety. This useless focus, moment-by-moment, extends into a continuum as days, months, years, whole lives go by.

Whatever your age, death will come to you in some way. Either young or old, by accident or sickness or some other means, death will certainly come.

Feeling completely prepared for death is very powerful. If we are fully prepared for death, then our life before death reflects that skillful and wise preparation.

Short moments is based on quantity, not quality. Any kind of perception of quality is subjective, so it means nothing. Quantity of short moments is key, just as a drop of water is key to filling an entire ocean.

All data, information and knowledge, however they shine forth, always glow as the unborn, all-creating essence. Whoever wants to instinctively recognize the essential meaning should recognize the all-creating essence.

Repetition furthers enlightened meaning experientially.

Generosity is the greatest gift.

Svābhāvikakāya—All-Pervasiveness—is not the way we have been taught to think, talk, live or to demonstrate ourselves in the world; however, that has nothing to say about whether it is the truth or not.

Great beings of the past, future and present are perfectly illuminated and empowered. Through igniting beneficial potency without effort, depend upon the living example of the victorious ones of all times.

Everyone here in this Teaching is here because they wish to be here. I'm a satisfaction of your reification, and you, mine!

Blissful buddha-hood—an ecosystem. Not a place somewhere, but our own intelligence-ecosystem that we are already in.

Living-buddhas come in many forms.

"I never move from inside perfect wisdom and have no place to find inside. I am sublime Bodhicitta without the mistake of otherness and without manifesting newly."

There is nothing greater than this. This is ultimate reality.

Everything appears vividly and is clearly illuminated within awareness. Nothing exists apart from the transcendent qualities of the primordial nature. There are no obstacles or blockages to this freedom.

We're not trying to get to anything or get away from anything. Everything, no matter what it is, is at ease.

The ultimate gift is to rest as loving open intelligence and to give spontaneously from that space of loving open intelligence.

Repetition furthers. The enlightenment of all is always already accomplished.

Anytime you're thinking about your Guru, you can be absolutely certain that your Guru is thinking about you.

You may analyze meticulously, but when a wind blows, it naturally disperses the clouds, and the sky can be seen. Endeavor to see empty lucidity, mind itself, in the same way—there is nothing greater than this understanding.

When death comes, ecstatically seize its clear light.

The thought of "wanting for others more than we wish even for ourselves" is an extraordinary and precious state and its occurrence a marvel unlike any other.

I didn't decide on Guru devotion, it decided on me!

The ultimate refuge—the true nature of my own mind of great bliss seeing emptiness—here I take refuge.

With freedom in immediate perception we relax. We see a thought come up and we see how quickly it releases on its own. It is emptiness taking itself to emptiness; there is no "thing" there anywhere.

The key point is the outshining of the ordinary mind.

Union with the Guru is perfect love of the Guru. Perfect love is love not dependent on conditions.

Love and devotion for the Guru is not personal.

Even though our present body and mind are not our identity, nevertheless, due to strong familiarity with reification, we directly and vividly see our identity as a separate body and mind. Because of this, whenever our body is unwell we say, "I am unwell," and whenever our mind is unhappy we say, "I am unhappy."

People with no experience of Dzogchen may find it difficult to believe that it is possible to change from believing oneself to be an ordinary person into being a buddha. But by developing a correct understanding of how persons lack true existence and are mere imputations, we realize that it is definitely possible.

Realization of buddha-body has been the experience of many millions of Dzogchen practitioners, not just a few here and there. *Millions* of Dzogchen practitioners have realized sublime being.

We are never separate from the buddhas of past, present and future, thus never apart from the Guru.

We are not findable. What is not findable is sublime. What is sublime is an inexhaustible treasury.

It is very important to understand that love and devotion to the Guru is not merely a person-to-person thing. It is not personal, like the love and devotion of one person for another. Everything is the Guru.

We are taught according to our desire and openness.

The Guru is only here to show the realization of ultimate Bodhicitta and sublime wisdom alive right now.

Our universe, even though we think it is very big, occupies a space no bigger than a subatomic particle, without the subatomic particle becoming bigger or the universe becoming smaller.

If the merit of Bodhicitta were to have form, it would be no smaller than the vessel that makes up the atmosphere of space.

The state of enlightenment means all personal aims have been totally accomplished. There's nothing more to achieve or attain, and so any activity is for the enlightenment of all, right now.

Repetition furthers. The enlightenment of all is always already accomplished.

Reification of data is outshone by the enlightened mind of great Bodhicitta bliss seeing emptiness.

The whole point of receiving and practicing the Teaching is to understand buddha-nature, which is the very essence of our being. We must be committed to realize our buddha-nature, even though we all already possess it. We must practice with joyous diligence to understand our own true nature. Nevertheless, we must remember that practice only reveals what is already present.

The buddha-essence is intrinsically present in all beings. It is not that some have it and some do not.

Without medicine even a very skillful doctor would find it difficult to cure illness. Similarly, without the medicine of Bodhicitta—the most important element of practice—it is difficult for practice to generate benefit.

Just as food provides strength to act in the world, ultimate Bodhicitta provides strength to follow the path to enlightenment and its qualities and activities. Nothing else can compare with it and nothing else will work. Whatever virtue or good you have accomplished, be it great or small, becomes measureless. All the negative you have accumulated in the past is instantly exhausted.

When we dedicate our life to the benefit of others, we naturally shed personal desires.

In the expanse of self-arisen wisdom, all possible reification—positive, negative and neutral—is originally perfect and primordially enlightened, with nothing to search for. The fluctuating reifications and ordinary perceptions liberate upon arising, vanishing naturally like night becomes day, and are established in the palace of the great primordial purity, fundamentally free.

Regardless of the total length of life, in each instant life is running out. The recognition of this impermanence is very important.

Mind of spontaneous great bliss seeing emptiness is equal to sublime open intelligence. Spontaneous great bliss is the main cause for attaining enlightenment. Even without attaining enlightenment, if there is just a taste of great bliss seeing emptiness, one will enjoy complete happiness.

The root of Bodhicitta is compassion. The principle method for developing compassion is contemplating the suffering of others and developing a wish to free all beings from their suffering. We need to allow this compassionate wish again and again until it arises spontaneously and then continuously influences all our thoughts and actions.

"To liberate all beings from their suffering, I must first attain enlightenment myself. Only then will I have the power to bring lasting enlightenment to all beings." This strong desire, rooted in compassion, to attain enlightenment to benefit all beings is Bodhicitta.

When falling asleep, there is a moment where it's clear that being awake is turning into sleep. In that moment of falling asleep, be alert to that instant and purposefully carry shining open intelligence into sleep. In this way, it's possible to realize that sleep is also a data stream.

Repetition furthers. The enlightenment of all is always already accomplished.

In what is called loving open intelligence, there are no opposites of good and bad and what is stated about them. Within loving open intelligence, within transition or change, endless appearances and possibilities, whether of good or bad, arise with nothing to renounce or attain.

Holy Guru, thank you for your supreme kindness. Through relying on you, all I attain is sublime open intelligence and love.

In the experience of those who do not perceive things through reification, the fact that things manifest without truly existing is so amazing. Although reified data does not exist, it manifests in all its variety. Although emptiness as a state does not exist, it extends infinitely, inexhaustibly, reaching everywhere. Although reification of good and bad does not exist, there can be fixation on things having description.

Loving open intelligence is focused and demonstrated in qualities and activities which ensure full enlightenment of the collective, quickly.

To free yourself from the cocoon of attachment to data, lay bare the all-penetrating mind of great bliss seeing emptiness and reveal explicitly its true nature.

Empowerment is the means by which a person is brought into the profound secrets of enlightenment and then given permission to engage in the practices relevant to them. The Twelve Empowerments contain a very clear explanation of empowerment and how it causes entrance into the indestructible vehicle of enlightenment and the enlightenment of all right now.

Those who are able to rest naturally, outshining the worship of thoughts, emotions and sensations, put aside the worldly cares and activities of this life and practice single-mindedly, gaining liberation—in this very lifetime—as great wisdom exaltation and sublime enlightened energy.

The mind, free of trying to do anything or stop anything is blissful, open, spacious and relaxed. How delightful to know the whole host of reification to be self-liberated. How happy it is when all reifications are self-liberated. When doubt neither arises nor ceases, doubt is self-liberated.

Attain enlightenment in this very life.

Printed in Great Britain
by Amazon